Stony Ground

Memoirs of a
theatrical
non-celebrity

Leslie Rocker

Published by New Generation Publishing in 2017

Copyright © Leslie Rocker 2017

First Edition

The author asserts the moral right under the Copyright, Designs and Patents Act 1988 to be identified as the author of this work.

All Rights reserved. No part of this publication may be reproduced, stored in a retrieval system or transmitted, in any form or by any means without the prior consent of the author, nor be otherwise circulated in any form of binding or cover other than that in which it is published and without a similar condition being imposed on the subsequent purchaser.

www.newgeneration-publishing.com

New Generation Publishing

Contents

Prologue 1

Chapter 1 – "The child is father to the man" 3

Chapter 2 – Shadow of a "great" war 8

Chapter 3 – School, trains, food and other matters 16

Chapter 4 - The war to end the war to end all wars 24

Chapter 5 – Dangerous daylight 30

Chapter 6 - Girls and boys come out to play 39

Chapter 7 – A troubling conflict 44

Chapter 8 - Upon a painted ocean 48

Chapter 9 - Down to the sea in a hulk 59

Chapter 10 – University of the sea 70

Chapter 11 - Ye olde order changeth 84

Chapter 12 – Magazines and plays 95

Chapter 13 - Our theatre in the 50s 102

Chapter 14 – Discovering poetry – and love 111

Chapter 15 - Golden days 115

Chapter 16 – Give me excess of it 125

Chapter 17 – An actor's life for me 136

Chapter 18 - The lure of the lights 143

Chapter 19 – Are you one of us? 151

Chapter 20 – The show must go on – or must it? 160

Chapter 21 – Resting 165

Chapter 22 – Auditions, schools and the Method 174

Chapter 23 - Camper than the campers 183

Chapter 24 – A wandering minstrel 190

Chapter 25 - "We'll be in love by the end of the season" 196

Chapter 26 – Back to the smoke 201

Chapter 27 - Actor manager 206

Chapter 28 – The ultimate goal 211

Chapter 29 - To be, then not to be 220

Epilogue 223

The author in the late 1950s. The picture was taken for publication in "Spotlight" the professional theatre's casting directory. A caption would have included details of age, theatre experience etc. and acting category, i.e. "character lead".

Prologue

"I should not talk so much about myself if there were anybody else whom I knew as well."
                                        Thoreau

I was a celebrity of sorts for about five minutes. I had a small speaking part in the soap opera Crossroads. This was in the days when most of the population of England tuned their television sets in to this new form of entertainment. I played the clerk of a court, appearing in several episodes. One of them was broadcast after my return to the rented room I then occupied in Clapham. I came downstairs the next morning to find a small group comprising my landlady and neighbours gathered on the steps outside the front door. When they saw me one said: "Oh! Mr Rocker, we didn't know you were a celebrity". I smiled and gave a wave like the Queen opening Parliament. Then I went on to my "resting" job sorting the Christmas mail.

This is a story covering a life with many vicissitudes and two obsessions: the live theatre and writing, which for reasons of length I have confined to the first 40 years. It is, of course, a personal account, but I hope some of it will have value as an historic record, involving as it does childhood poverty in the 1920s and 1930s, London in the blitz and life as a conscripted merchant seaman. For the same reason I have included a detailed account of culture in the 1950s, which for me represents the end of an era. Those who are not interested in the music, drama and other artistic activities of the decade, however, may wish to skip those chapters and follow the narrative through a career in journalism and magazine editing; amateur dramatics in the East End; provincial rep. and touring; until the final goal is reached on the West End stage.

Chapter 1 – "The child is father to the man"

My enthusiasm for, and love of, the live theatre was initiated by an experience at about the age of three, presumably in 1930. My older sister had a friend who at one time, almost unbelievably considering the family's cramped living conditions, came to live with us and shared her room. They were kind to me and on a memorable occasion took me to a pantomime. It was at London's Lyceum Theatre, then famous for this form of show. It is interesting to reflect that even the poorest at that time could afford an evening at a top West End venue that nowadays is probably the privilege only of tourists and the relatively opulent.

It was an immeasurably grand affair. The text of the story (I think it was Cinderella) was printed in verse and included in the programme. At one point children were invited to the stage by the clowns in the *commedia del 'arte* to be showered with sweets. Then there were the transformation scenes with sheet after glittering sheet of bespangled wonder rising up into what I now know was the flies, but then thought was heaven.

The next morning I awoke in floods of tears. My sister and mother were unable to console me. What, they asked, was the matter? Didn't I like the show? The bedroom was dark, the window a kind of double door opening out into a paved gap between the terrace houses. It had a red blind that when pulled down suffused the room in a sanguine glow. I gazed at my dismal surroundings and through my sobs and my misery could only try to explain: "It will never happen again". And in a way it never did.

Looking back to one's childhood so many decades ago is like reading someone else's diary from which pages have been torn – perhaps deliberately. Those memories that remain are not necessarily high-lights. Freud might give them a significance they certainly do not deserve.

Modern psychiatrists might believe the other entries to be repressed, rather than simply forgotten. I can only present them as them as they come to mind It is both a personal record and a history of periods in a life.

A recent article in the national press suggested that "most of us can't recall" their earliest years. I certainly remember some incidents vividly and no doubt they have been formative of my later development. Sometimes in the cause of honesty it may be necessary to relate matters that are unsavoury and my very first memory is one of these. I was lying alone in my parents' bed. I'm not sure why I was there. Usually I slept with my brother Eric in another bed in the same room. I would have been about two years of age. I leaned over, lifted up the sheets and blankets and peered below. There was a large chamber pot, which I pulled out and looked in. Something in it was red and white and vaguely unpleasant. I returned it hastily. Only now, writing these notes, do I find myself associating this with Molly Bloom.

My brother was my senior by four years. My sister, Edna, who slept in an adjoining room, eleven years older. Our family rented the ground floor of a three storey Victorian house in the north London suburb of Wood Green. It comprised the two bedrooms; a tiny combined eating and living room that for some reason was called the "kitchen"; and a scullery, which contained a chipped stone sink, gas stove and a walk-in food store, misnamed the "pantry".

At some stage an elderly lady lived on the middle floor. She was quite feeble and had some kind of muscular fault that caused the thumb on one of her hands to tremble. I remember little of her, although I occasionally spent time talking to her. At some time she was replaced by a family that occupied all the rooms on that floor and one of those above.

Another brother, Frederick (more usually Fred), slept in the other of the rooms on the top floor. He was born on the eleventh day of the eleventh month, 1911. The figure 1 was regarded in the family as having some significance, my father's birthday being on 1 January and our house number 11. I have a brief image of Fred as a recalcitrant teenager, sprawling with his legs out in the tiny living room.

There was no electricity, of course. Rooms were lit by gas served through funny little "mantles" that burned with a yellowish light. As an economy measure the gas was not used in all the rooms and I went to bed with the light from candles, which flickered and made reading difficult, probably contributing to my poorer eyesight later in life.

Under the house was a cellar, not high enough to stand up in, the only light a small grating looking out to the street. Coal was delivered down a winding flight of stone steps through a door that was scarcely big enough to admit both the coalman and his load. There were three types of fuel: best nuts, nutty slack and coke, piled in different areas of the murky, spider-ridden hole. Some of those who delivered the coal, crouching down under their hundredweight loads, were little more than children, with yellow teeth gritted through their blackened faces. They wore strange leather caps on their heads, with flaps down the back to protect their necks.

The lavatory was let into the back wall of the house and reached through the garden. The seat was a fixed length of wood with a hole in it. We could not afford toilet paper and anyway my father scoffed at such an indulgence, maintaining it was unnecessary for normal toiletry processes. Squares of newspaper were cut, threaded with string and hung on a nail. Fortunately, printer's ink had less of a tendency to lift from the page in those days.

The kitchen table was of scrubbed wood and could be extended to admit extra panels, seldom used. It was covered with a chenille cloth, over which a cotton tablecloth was spread for meals. A presiding memory is of being instructed to "shake the cloth" outside the back door to rid it of crumbs.

In one corner of the room was an easy chair with

wooden arms and a prevailing image is of my father sitting with his legs stretched out on another chair and our two cats on his lap. He read books. They were mainly crime fiction, with an occasional Western. He obtained them from what was known as a circulating library. He did not choose them himself, presumably because the effort of walking the mile or so to the High Street was more that he was prepared to undertake. I was sent to ask for the next available title. "The lady will know what I want", he would say.

He smoked, of course. Nearly everybody did in those days (except, strangely, my mother) and the habit was encouraged by the images projected on to the cinema screens. His favoured brand was Craven A, an unpopular choice for me as it was the only one that did not carry "cigarette cards", which my friends were able to collect and barter. The cigarettes were described as corked-tip, although they had no filter, merely a piece of brown foil at the mouth end. Sometime during my childhood I suffered from a disorder that was diagnosed as catarrh. I was taken to the doctor, where my mother asked: "Is there any cure?"

"Oh! no", came the reply. "He will probably have it all his life". Fortunately, I did not. The idea of a smoking related illness would not arise for many years to come, but the habit unquestioningly shortened my father's life by anything up to 20 years.

I learnt to read early, before I went to school, and remember one rare moment of contiguity with my father sitting on his knee and reading Tom and the Water Babies. This was my favourite book, which I devoured many times. The image of the little boy diving into the river and having the sooty grime from life's chimneys husking from his new clean body was obviously not without its resonance in my life.

One day I was taken to the famous Regents Park zoo. This was a staple form of entertainment for the Londoner then. Involving no more expense than a trip on a tram and a low price entry fee, it was one diversion that those in our financial situation could afford. The first time we went I encountered a wonder: it was a huge beast caparisoned in crimson and gold and surmounted by a gilded chariot bearing god-like people who shouted and waved. It was called an elephant and I stood enchanted as it strode with its long, majestic steps through my life.

I have no idea how long it was before I was taken again, when we did the rounds of the animals, including the lions and the tigers and the monkeys and the parrots. We started to leave, but I said I wanted to see the elephant. My parents told me I had seen it. I disagreed. After a brief argument we went back to look at a grey creature staring out at us from behind the bars of a cage. There! They said. That's an elephant. No it's not, I said. I want to see the elephant. I was taken to the exit, but made such a fuss they took me back to the cage. Where was my vision in crimson and gold? They carried me kicking and screaming from the park and we never went again.

Quite early my brother Fred moved out of the house and Eric and I were able to move into his room on the top floor. At last I had a bed to myself. Nights were certainly more comfortable, but I was obviously still a rather troubled child. One day my father took me to visit Fred, who was living in a room above Burtons, the tailors, in Wood Green High Street. He was lying on his bed looking very poorly, but my father had little sympathy for such weakness. He was disgusted at the state of the room and its occupant and advised him to "pull himself together". Later that illness was diagnosed as epilepsy. It developed into dementia and had a severe impact not only on his life but also on those of my parents and to a lesser extent myself.

Chapter 2 – Shadow of a "great" war

The brooding presence of my father pervaded our lives. He had served in Flanders during World War 1 and talked about it little, except to drop dark hints occasionally about gas attacks and bombardments. It has been called the Great War, but in my view there was nothing great about it, except the vast numbers of dead and the millions of young men who spent the rest of their lives suffering from various mental and physical disabilities.

Serving in it would even have affected those who, like my father, could be said to have had a "good" war. He was uninjured and rose in the ranks to become company sergeant major. There are pictures of a proud, moustachioed man in uniform. But you can't take four years out of a young man's life and expect him to return to normality back in "blighty". Something happened to change a man so obviously capable of achievement into the disillusioned, dilatory person I remember with such clarity and sadness.

He was offered a commission if he was prepared to stay on in Europe after the war, but he chose to come home to what was then a young family. As a non-commissioned officer I think he may have become accustomed to absolute obedience in the men under his command and probably found it difficult to adjust to normal relationships with his children. My memory suggests he was constantly at odds with my brothers although Eric's recollections are of a much more sympathetic relationship. He was certainly not a violent man, but the mental tyranny he seemed to impose on me weighed heavily throughout my childhood.

He was capable of disproportionate acts of retribution. Once he gave me two pennies, my first pocket money. I think I was about four. I immediately went to the local toy shop and bought a miniature pack of playing cards. The adults played cards at home and these would be my own special pack. When he came home from work I showed them to him proudly. "Where did you get the money for those?" he demanded. I told him. "I gave you that to buy a piggy bank so that you could save money. I will never give you any pocket money again". And he didn't.

Rather more serious was his extraordinary attitude towards my sister. One day when I was very young he pointed to the model of a sailing ship on top of a shed. He told me it had been made by German prisoners of war. "I brought that back for my baby daughter", he said. "But when I got home I found I had no baby daughter". According to my mother he had not spoken to my sister for 15 years. I wondered what terrible sin she had committed to bring such a fate on her head, particularly as she was born in 1916 and would only have been three years of age when he ostracised her.

My mother seemed totally submissive and I do not recall any demonstration of love between her and my father. What affection he was capable of was lavished on a dog. It was a cross-breed, supposedly something between a collie and a whippet. His name was Toby, but for some reason he was always called "Pup". My father adored him. He regarded him as supremely intelligent and taught him tricks that were shown off to guests on the rare occasions we had "company". My role was to assist.

It was also my appointed task to walk it regularly, a chore I hated and no doubt led to my aversion of the canine breed throughout my life. My father would complain that it was not given enough exercise, although he contributed little to it himself. The dog died when quite young and my father was heart-broken. He blamed me for not exercising it enough and buried it in the tiny back-garden, refusing to say whereabouts. After that I used to have an unpleasant dream in which I believed I was responsible for somebody's death and had buried the body. Many years later, when I had returned to live at the family home, I dug up the oppressive ivy and Virginia creeper that covered the rear of the house and found the bones of the dog and – sceptics may scoff if they will – never had that dream again.

My father thought of himself as a handyman and was particularly keen on carpentry, at which he was curiously inept. This was partly due to his inadequate equipment: rusting saw, hammer with a loose head, screwdrivers with bent shafts, blunt chisels with tiny notches in the blades. When we had snow he made a sledge, but used three-by-two timber for the runners, with the result it was altogether too heavy. Near the top of a run it buried itself and covered the rider with freezing snow. Then one summer he made a kite, but again used trellis lathes that would not let it get off the ground. Later, when the board game Monopoly became the rage he made up his own version with crude drawings and lettering on a sheet of plywood and money cut from coloured paper. Somehow, it lacked charm and we had to wait some time before we acquired the original.

In the early 1930s unemployment was in the millions and my father seldom held a job for long. He had at one time been a butcher, but hated the work largely because of the immeasurably long hours. He sometimes called himself a salesman, which meant that he delivered groceries door to door, a not-uncommon practice at that time. One such company was called Carwadines, of which he used to say that its head office was number one London, being located at 1 Ludgate Hill. One day he came home and said he had a job at a remarkable new factory in Tottenham called Wonderloaf where steam-baked bread was produced, sliced and wrapped on a continuous flow-line. We didn't know it at the time, but it was the beginning of the modern world of pre-packed foods.

My mother wandered through it all with a resigned look on her face, supplementing the family income with what was then called charring, although this was illegal while my father was "on the dole". Shabby, ill-dressed, constantly aproned or "overalled", she wore her stockings wrinkled around her ankles [like Nora Batty!]. She knitted, but not very well and I remember going to school in an ill-fitting "pullover" with no arms, presumably because my mother had run out of wool!

I had a rich uncle, Fred, who lived in a fine house in the posh district of Southgate. Although you had to be well-off in those days to own a car, he ran two, one I believe an Austin 7 with a drop-head, and the other a little two-seater with a rumble seat. His money came from a meat processing factory that was located only a few hundred yards from where we lived. My father never mentioned him, spoke to him, or visited him either in his factory or his family home, despite the fact that his brother could presumably have offered him work during his long periods of unemployment.

My mother would visit his wife Emily, who also happened to be her sister. My cousin, Ethel, would drive us, another cousin, May, and her children out into the surrounding countryside of Hertfordshire, where we picnicked on the grass and paddled in a little stream. Those were rare blissful days. At Christmas I would be taken to see their Christmas tree, which was very grand and spangled with lights. There were presents under the tree, but I cannot recollect ever being given one.

The family that lived in the middle floor moved out and we acquired the whole house, for a rent that was, I believe, 7s. 6d a week. I was sorry to see them go. They had a couple of daughters and a son a little older than me and I have a recollection of childish orgies in which we played doctors and nurses and performed mildly obscene operations on our naked bodies. I suppose nowadays such activities would be regarded as in some way delinquent, but it all seems very innocent looking back on it now. Children, it seems, need to have the opportunity of experimenting with the extraordinary physical characteristics they have been given to carry through their lives.

The change greatly improved our living conditions. I now at last had a room to myself. We even had a bathroom, although without hot water. Previously, bathing had taken place in a tin bath. This was at one time sited in the tiny scullery. Once I was standing naked in the bath washing myself when my mother picked up a pan of boiling water from the adjacent gas stove. She carried it towards the sink, but spilt it down my bare back. I screamed and can remember the incident clearly, but curiously have no recollection of the pain. Apart from being wrapped in sheeting I can't recall having any treatment, or visiting a hospital or doctor.

After that the tin bath was located in the living room, where in the winter I was warmed by the fire in the kitchen range. This was a device that may still be seen in Victorian houses to this day. A coke fire burned beside an oven, which to my knowledge my mother never used for cooking. Adults bathed in the public baths located alongside the local indoor swimming pool.

By now my sister had left home and the room she occupied was turned into a "drawing" room. The room I had slept in earlier became a dining room, furnished with the obligatory table and four chairs. We even acquired a piano. Although an upright, this nevertheless seemed very grand to us. It came from a well-known piano supplier of the time called Boyd. An inscription in the lid stated that the wood had been taken from a tree reputedly planted by Queen Elizabeth the First, although how anybody knew was not clear. Even the poorest in those days owned a piano – usually paid for, as ours would have been, on a "never-never", credit scheme. It constituted one of the principal forms of entertainment for people in their own homes.

My mother came from quite a musical family. Cousins of hers had had their own ensemble quite celebrated in its day comprising only members of the family under the name Imeson. She played a limited range of music, her favourite being Sinding's Rustle of Spring. When we had "company" she would render popular songs of the day, such as: "It's a sin to tell a lie", "When I grow too old to dream", and "When the poppies bloom again". I was encouraged to sing them. My brother Eric, perhaps envious, would sneer at my efforts and say: "He can't sing".

Looking back it seems that our living conditions were tolerable and I certainly would not want this to be regarded as just another childhood misery account. Indeed, my parents seemed to regard our family as on a social and economic level above what is now regarded as "working class" I suppose we could be described as living in "genteel poverty". I suspect conditions were not much worse than they are for the poorest today. £3 a week was regarded as the minimum on which a family could survive and the unemployment pay was, I believe £2.10.00 (that is at 20 shillings to the pound). One great advantage we had then over a present-day family, of course, was that there was no pressure to spend money on the appurtenances of modern life.

Food was cheap, particularly the basics that today can be disproportionately expensive. Looking back from our modern urban environments with their shop-less estates, featureless neighbourhoods and distant car-driven supermarkets it is astonishing to recall the shopping facilities we enjoyed at that time. The little street we lived in had about eight houses. It was divided in the middle by a street in which the local Post Office sorting office was located, complete with public telephones. Beyond this road was a row of shops, including, if my memory serves me correctly, a greengrocer, cobbler, hairdresser, confectioner/tobacconist, newsagent/stationer and public house. This proliferation was only partly due to the fact that they were adjacent to a station on the main line railway to the north, which had its own little row of satellite retail outlets, including another tobacconist and a separate sweet shop.

We talked about "round the back" or "over the bridge", where the road crossed the railway line. There must have been twenty or so shops and I was often sent there, clutching pennies, to buy the occasional loaf of bread or something from the hardware merchant. Milk was, of courses, delivered to the house on a horse-drawn "float".

The jewel in the crown, however, was Wood Green High Street, regarded as one of the finest in suburban London and only about a mile away, easy walking distance for us then. At either end of the street there was an Underground station; trams and buses ran along it, stopping at convenient intervals; cars were few and parking not, therefore, a problem. This ensured a substantial influx of customers from other boroughs such as Hornsey, Harringay, Palmers Green, Southgate and Tottenham.

All the top national retailers were represented: Woolworths, Marks and Spencer, British Home Stores, Burtons and Fifty-Shilling Tailors. There was a proliferation of women's clothing shops, one or two men's "outfitters", many shoe shops, some of them side by side. There were food shops galore: butchers, fishmongers, greengrocers, provision shops such as Sainsburys and Home and Colonial. Competition among them was intense, so prices were kept to a minimum. I would help my mother carry the weekly supplies home in paper carrier bags with string handles threaded through little cardboard tubes.

There being no electricity, we had nothing to burn up our tiny resources. We listened to the radio, or wireless as it was called then. This was powered by batteries, which had to be charged by a curious device called an accumulator, which in turn had to be renewed at a local hardware shop. We boiled water in kettles on the ancient gas stove or the kitchen range in the winter. Washing up was in the scullery sink, with the one cold tap.

As a family we only ever went on holiday once, to the seaside resort of Margate, where the principal attraction was a fair ground called Dreamland. It was not a happy occasion. We stayed in a poor little boarding house. My brother and I must have misbehaved because my father said "never again" and we never did.

We had day trips to Southend, where there was a lighted fairy land and the world's longest pier, but somehow they had little appeal. As a result I have never felt the need or the desire to indulge in the modern obsession with holiday making. Although strangely whenever I have visited an English seaside town in later life there is something in the deepest part of my consciousness that still recalls the smell of Brussel sprouts emanating through boarding house windows. Thus do the shadows we cast as children stay with us and lengthen as the days draw in.

Chapter 3 – School, trains, food and other matters

I was taken to my first infant school not by my mother, but by my teen-age sister. It was obviously a traumatic experience as I remember having to be carried kicking and screaming into the class. But they were very kind there and life must have been fairly equable because I have no recollections of it at all.

All of the children in our family went to the "infant" and "junior" schools affiliated to the parish church of St Michael's, from which they took their name. All the teachers were female and the schools were generally regarded as offering the best education in the district, although my mother always suspected that pupils whose parents were regular church attendees were favoured over those who were not. I do not think there was any justification for this. Indeed, although they were what nowadays would be regarded as "faith" schools, I do not recall that there was any attempt to influence pupils towards Christianity, except for the occasional visit to church on special occasions.

In the" junior" school I had two close friends – John Ingleby and Alec Latter – there, I can remember their names to this day. We fought and played together. John's parents had a small grocer's shop and he used to steal small triangles of cream cheese, which we ate in the bushes of the various open spaces available to us. There was also a "swing" park with the usual appurtenances, including slides and swings of different heights, seesaws and a monster creature like a bucking bronco. Nobody, to my recollection, had any accidents or serious falls despite the concrete surface.

At the age of 11 I would normally have expected to sit for the examination that, if I passed, would qualify me for attendance at a grammar school. Discussions took place, however, on whether this was the best course for me. I do not remember being consulted and a decision was taken that probably had a major impact on my life and denied me the possibility of achieving a formal university education. So despite what must have been my obvious leaning towards an academic turn of mind it was decided that I should take advantage of a new educational process just being introduced.

Instead of sitting the exam at 11, I would continue at ordinary state school and, if I passed a modest test at 14, would attend one of the newly established technical colleges. These provided a three-year course of vocational training in such subjects as carpentry, metalwork, engineering, etc. or a two-year commercial course, which included book-keeping, typewriting, Pitman's shorthand, English, Spanish and what were entitled Industrial History and Commercial Geography. One of these colleges was located in the nearby borough of Tottenham, replacing what had formerly been a "polytechnic".

So from the age of 12 I attended one of the local senior schools, Alexandra, which had a poor reputation academically and socially. I had hoped to be accepted at a better one called Bounds Green and I remember my deep disappointment when I opened the letter informing me of the decision. My close friend Ken, who was a little older than me, was a pupil there. He lived a curious life. His mother owned and ran a tiny tobacconist's shop near the station, to which he would carry hot food that had been cooked in their home, a flat located some distance away. His father had a good job in the editorial department of a famous national magazine in central London, to which he travelled every day. He was held in awe by us children because he was reputed to have fallen down the escalator in Leicester Square underground station, apparently the longest in the world. It was believed he only survived because he was a short man with a very short neck!

As it turned out Alexandra was not so bad. One Christmas the decision was made to produce "A Christmas Carol". We read the script and I became very excited at the possibility that I might play Scrooge. For days and weeks beforehand I walked about, wringing my hands and saying how mean I was. In the event Ken got the part, possibly because his father was responsible for having the scripts typed. I was given the part of Tiny Tim and had only to hobble on to the stage with a crutch at the end of the play and intone: "God Bless Us Everyone". It was my first speaking part!

One day the whole school was called together for what was a relatively rare full assembly. We had been presented with a wonderful new piece of equipment. It was called a radiogram and could play gramophone records - in those days 78 rpm. A teacher put on a record. She explained it was a piece of what was called classical music and wrote the composer's name "Hayden" on a blackboard. One of her colleagues corrected this to "Hyden". A short altercation followed, during which alternatives were suggested by other teachers. I had seen the name on a sheet of music on my mother's piano, so very bravely I put my hand up and told them what to their surprise and chagrin they realised was the correct spelling!

So a school that found time and space to introduce classical music to its pupils and encourage them to indulge in a stage play based on a Dickens story could not have been all bad.

When I was nine I wrote my first novel. I had been introduced to mystery stories through the pages of the Strand Magazine, of which my aunt had the first dozen bound volumes containing, of course, the Sherlock Holmes stories. Mine was called the "Limestone Murder Mystery". I showed it to my parents and my teachers, none of whom were particularly impressed. I received encouragement, however, from a teacher at the non-denominational Sunday school I attended. She typed the little manuscript and provided it with a cover, and stapled it. She even inserted a frontispiece showing a picture of "Limestone Mansion". I still have it somewhere and bless her to this day. When my aunt died I inherited those precious green volumes of the Strand, but they have since gone astray and would no doubt be worth a considerable sum now.

My parents would go to the cinema once a week, usually on a Monday and always took me with them. At some stage I tried my hand at film criticism. This took the form of a tabulated list showing date, cinema, name of film, its stars and my comments, confined to single graphic words, ranging from the best – superb, or smashing, - via excellent and very good, down to rubbish and tripe. They were followed by a monthly review, running to all of 100 words. Perhaps inevitably, the films that seemed to achieve the highest accolades were those with themes of adventure or thrills. The North-West Mounted Police, for example, staring Gary Cooper and two of the top teen-age female heart-throbs, Madeleine Carrol and Paulette Goddard. It reached the ultimate in praise with "superb", "smashing" and "marvellous". I was also particularly impressed with a programme that included not only Paul Muni as the founder of the Hudson Bay Company ("superb"), but also a "smashing" Night Train to Munich, with Rex Harrison.

It is said that people who live adjacent to parks and open places generally enjoy a better quality of life than those who do not and this was partly true of us children. Some of the green spaces, especially the smaller decorative gardens, such as one appropriately called the "Rose Gardens", were surrounded by railings with gates that were religiously padlocked every night. Signs told everyone to keep off the grass and a park-keeper would emerge angrily from his lair to chase any small boys who dared to transgress. The "parkie" had a sinister-looking spike on the end of a stick for picking up litter. It filled us with dread, but it was diverting to bait him and experience the thrill of the chase. Our house overlooked one of the gardens and Ironically despite the concern over the pristine lawns and tidy shrubberies a few years later in World War 2 the railings were removed – to make into bullets, they said – and the grass was dug up for an air-raid shelter.

There were also larger parks, such as Broomfield and Grovelands, in neighbouring boroughs, where we used to congregate, reaching them by bicycle. They had boating lakes, rudimentary tennis courts and areas where we could play football. The Alexandra Palace was within walking distance of my home. We loved to play in the grounds, especially when the grass was cut and there was hay to throw about, pile up and roll in. A little single-decker tram trundled up the hill from the main shopping centre, stopped at the gates to the grounds, turned round and went back again, unless there was an event like a ball in the Great Hall, when it continued on up to the Palace itself.

The building was little used, however, and in a state of disrepair. It was said that the four towers on each corner might have to be removed for safety reasons. Then one of them was replaced by a new and marvellous metal structure. We learnt that from it moving pictures could be radiated to people's homes, although we regarded it as a novelty that would never catch on. Later the little tram became a bus, a road was cut through the grounds and Wood Green was linked for the first time with its rather grander neighbour Muswell Hill.

As a child it seemed my life was dominated by railways. At one end of the terrace I lived in was Wood Green Station on the London and North Eastern Railway (LNER) main line from Kings Cross to Edinburgh. At the other end Palace Gates, also LNER, was the terminus of a branch line from Liverpool Street and the London docks. Beyond this there was a marshalling yard where trucks were loaded and unloaded and sent out on their journeys. At night I used to lie in bed and hear the noise of the trains creating a symphony of sound: the big drums of the expresses passing through on their way to the North; the pizzicato of the goods trains clambering up an incline; the local trains whistling at their stops and starts.

Sitting on the roof of a shed by the main line a few of us collected train numbers. Those were the days of the great Pacific class expresses, which later became streamlined, first for the Jubilee – the Silver King, Silver Fox, etc - then in blue for the Coronation – Empire of India, Republic of South Africa, Commonwealth of Australia – and finally in green with the great Mallard, fastest steam train in the world. They all had names and when we saw one rushing through with its great plume of steam, we noted it with its number. I had almost completed the list when I lost my book, or it was stolen. I gave up then. We watched the "semaphore" signals that told us when an express was approaching and would call out to our fellows; "eccy Scots", or "eccy Kings" accordingly.

The path we followed to get to the shed went further on to a remote swimming pool, where men could swim in the nude, with one day set aside for ladies only. It was kept free of contamination by painting the walls of the pool with lime wash and I seem to recollect a shed where the pile of lime was kept to be shovelled into the pool when required.

The trains from Palace Gates ran to Seven Sisters, where they linked with the Great Eastern Railway and Liverpool Street station in central London. Many years later I was attending a press conference on board a ship in King George V Dock when I encountered a railway station. To my astonishment I found that the trains from it ran to the station a few yards from my home. I boarded one and was taken on a magical mystery ride through parts of London I never knew existed, past the ends of people's gardens, where inhabitants would wave to us as we passed. That all came to an end when a man named Beeching attempted to improve the health of an industry by killing it.

For a penny we could buy a return ticket for a journey from Wood Green to the next stations on the line: Hornsey in one direction, or Hatfield (more attractive because it meant going through a tunnel) in the other. For the same money it was also possible to travel all day on the trams, and once we got as far as Woolwich, where we spent another penny to travel across the Thames and back on a ferry, eating a meat pie we bought from a stall.

What we ate would probably be regarded with horror by the children of today, but we walked, we cycled, and despite what would nowadays be regarded as deprivation we were healthy. I was so thin that even my father made jokes about my legs hanging like ribbons from my short trousers. But I fought and romped with the other boys and nobody bullied me.

The dietary routine at home was fairly rigid, but obviously nourishing. On Sunday we had a joint of meat, leg of lamb alternated with aitchbone of beef (sold and cooked off the bone). The vegetables were mainly roast potatoes, cooked under the joint in its fat, or separately in "lard", cabbage crushed to a pulp, and a pulse called butter beans. For dessert there was suet pudding, either spotted dick with sultanas or plain served with syrup. The suet for the puddings was bought in a lump from the butcher and grated.

On Monday we ate the meat cold with "bubble and squeak" fried from the remains of the vegetables. On Tuesday the meat was reheated in a kind of stew, which possibly served us for two days. Any meat left could be made into rissoles. Then there were sausages and fish and chips (the fish bought fresh, dipped in our own batter and deep fried). There was no such thing as a take-away, except for fish and chips, and we never, but never, went out to a restaurant or pub.

We ate sweets of course. They were available in abundance and very cheap. It's a wonder any of us kept our teeth into adulthood. The gob stoppers, bulls' eyes, toffees were stored in large glass jars on the shelves of confectioners, tipped into scales and served in little paper bags. The owner of a tobacconist and confectioner in our street also owned a small lock-up shop near the station where only confectionery was sold. It was managed by a young woman who made herself popular with us boys by giving us over the weight in sweets and sometimes not taking our money at all.

One day she invited some of us to the room she rented,

where she lay on the bed, lifted her skirt and allowed us to encounter her sexual secrets. She seemed to enjoy the excitement this aroused in us and the tactile experiments it encouraged. She said we could come back another day for what she intimated would be something even more appealing, but whether it happened or not I do not know for I was not involved again. Looking back it is apparent that we were in physical as well as moral danger. Nowadays it would no doubt be regarded as a form of abuse, but I doubt if it made any serious impact on any of us.

Chapter 4 - The war to end the war to end all wars

When I was 12 it was decided that I should learn to play the piano and my brother Fred agreed to teach me. He played brilliantly and I can still see him to this day sitting at the keyboard with the dedicated concentration of the talented performer. His forte was Chopin and Liszt, and a particular favourite of his was the Lieberstraum. He also constantly played a melodic little piece called Alice Where Art Thou, which seemed to haunt the household and perhaps reflected something of his psychological state.

He had married, quite well it seemed, and rented a flat in the up-market suburb of Muswell Hill, furnishing it with a grand piano and other furniture that my mother regarded as the height of extravagance. To reach it I had to walk the two or three miles through the grounds of Alexandra Palace. There I had my first lesson and learnt to play scales. When the lesson was over there was a radio broadcast by the Prime Minister, Neville Chamberlain. He had solemn words for us. The country was at war with Germany. This was not entirely unexpected. The surprise came immediately afterwards when the air-raid siren sounded.

We knew about the bombing in Poland. We had been warned to prepare for it in England. We had been issued with gas masks in little cardboard boxes that in the event of war being declared we were to keep with us at all times. But when I left home war had not been declared. Now here I was, several miles away, without it. What should we do? Damp towels, for our faces perhaps? A rug against the living room door? And how should we take cover if the bombs started falling? Air raid shelters had not by then been built or dug.

Fortunately, within a very short time the All Clear sounded. Perhaps the warning had been a wake-up call. There might be another warning, however, before I could reach the relative safety of my home so needless to say I covered the distance in record time. It was the last as well as the first of my piano lessons, something I have regretted all my life. Looking back it is curious that my mother never attempted to teach me how to play, or about music generally, despite the fact that she presumably had sufficient skill.

So began five years of war: five years of turmoil in the world around us, in the skies over our heads; five years of a blacked-out city; five years of rationed food, of coupons for clothing, of cold winter mornings spent planting seed potatoes in an allotment; five years of newspaper headlines, and wireless reports, and cinema newsreels; five years watching the enemy advancing ever closer across the continent of Europe - the destruction of Poland, the annexation of Austria, Czechoslovakia, the fall of Paris, the retreat from Dunkirk. Then hope at last with the first great victories in North Africa, the Italian campaign, the arrival of the Americans, the Allies' invasion of Europe.

And all that time life went on. As children we still went to school, although we took some work home when the air-raids were persistent. Many children were evacuated from London to rural areas. I was not. Parents were given a choice. My mother, who was not known for rationality, decided arbitrarily that she wanted to "keep the family together". "If one goes, we all go", she said. In fact, as she was often out to work and my father was involved in the Civil Defence this meant that I was often alone in the house during the daylight raids, or with my elder brother, Fred.

My mother's curious concept of fatality also led to our never going down an air-raid shelter. "What will be, will be", she said. My father spent some time reinforcing the cellar beneath our house with stout beams, lining the walls with plywood, installing a bed, table and candle in a little glass container. After it was completed my mother went down there, but came back minutes later. There were spiders there, she said, and never went down again!

The little park overlooked by our house was dug up for an air-raid shelter and I would watch local residents with their bedding and provisions queuing for a place in the dank, dark tunnels. Then I would go to bed in my room on the top floor of our tall house overlooking London and sleep through the worst the Hun could throw at us. We were, perhaps, fortunate in the northern suburbs. Had we lived south of the city perhaps we might have taken a different view. It was thought that some German pilots preferred to drop their loads of death as soon as they had reached the southern outskirts of London, which were known as Bomb Alley.

Then the Germans introduced a new device, one that did not rely on an explosive detonation to cause the maximum devastation. It was an incendiary bomb, dropped *en masse,* that ignited fires when it fell. One night my blackout curtain glowed red, the light around the edges so bright that I could not sleep. I got up and pulled the curtain aside. The southern sky was ablaze and, although it was some 12 miles away, I could distinctly see the flames shooting up from the blazing dockland. A few days later I took the tube to the centre of London and walked through the rubble and broken glass that had once been our proud city.

The night raids were intended to destroy our commercial and industrial heartlands, our means of communication and our morale. By day the Germans had a different strategy: to achieve mastery in the skies. It was the Battle of Britain. For the first time war could be watched by people on the ground in the southern counties, or by the rest of us on newsreels in the cinema. Without realising it, we were living through history that children might watch decades later on television sets.

Bravely and successfully though our pilots fought, many bombers got through. On one occasion I was spending a quiet Sunday afternoon with my parents in our front living room when we heard the sound of an aircraft. There had been no alarm so we assumed it was "one of ours". However the sound of the engine was unfamiliar. I went to the front door and looked out. It was a dull autumn day and suddenly out of the low clouds a plane emerged. I could tell from the cross on its fuselage that it was a German bomber.

It circled the house and I hastened to the back to try and catch another glimpse. It had turned and now came back on its path, obviously lining up along the railway. Looking up I could see the pilot's face quite clearly. Could he see mine? Did we for a tiny moment confront one another, harbinger of death about to release the weapons of war, small boy looking up in curiosity and awe?

I went back to the front door and watched it fly south. A few shapes fell from its belly, so slowly that for a moment I wondered if they were parachutists. The bombs straddled the railway line, causing much damage and a few casualties. We knew of a blind lady who lived nearby and who would walk past our house with the aid of a white stick and sometimes leaning on the arm of a young man, who was her brother. He was crossing the railway on a footbridge when the bombs struck and was never heard of again.

The sound of falling bombs could be a terrifying experience, but somehow we came to accept it as part of the pattern of war, together with the boom of anti-aircraft guns and the metallic ping of the shrapnel from their shells. As we listened to the whine of the falling bombs we waited for the successive crunches, one, two, three, four, five, six. They straddled the house, but fortunately fell either side of it. A mano-second of time in the release of the stick and it would be our body and those of our family that were being dug out of the ruins by the Civil Defence team in the next few hours.

What I found to be more frightening was what was known as the parachute bomb. These were land-mines that floated down silently from the marauding aircraft to land softly and gently in, perhaps, a residential area. I remember lying awake at night wondering if a quiet death was that very moment spreading its shroud in the back garden. They were more destructive than single high-explosive bombs, because whereas those would penetrate the ground, destroying a house and perhaps one or two neighbours each side, the mines remained on the surface, their explosive force free to devastate properties for yards, even miles, around. My father took me to nearby Chingford, where he had an acquaintance. There was no sign of his friend's house, or of his street, or of many in its neighbourhood.

We knew the Germans were an ingenious enemy. We saw it as part of their villainy! There were rumours of secret weapons and one day what was called the V1 appeared. It was a pilotless, radio- controlled aircraft, a funny little device, like a child's toy, but no plaything. It flew with a loud buzzing noise and the British, being British, laughed at it and gave it a funny name: a Doodle-bug. I watched one cross the sky one night when walking the five miles home from a girl friend's house in Enfield, having missed the last trolley bus. It travelled along the distant horizon, trailing its little plume of fire: man's intruder on my night sky, through the Plough and the Pleiades.

A way was found to deal with it tactically during the day. Fighter pilots flew close and tipped its wing so that it could be turned off-course. On the ground we learnt that it was safe so long as the noise continued. When that cut out we knew the device would be spiralling towards the ground and, of course, to those immediately underneath.

One day I was in central London, crossing Broadway towards St James's Park Station. I realised that I seemed to be alone in the street. I looked around and saw that people were sheltering in office doorways or even lying on the ground. A Doodle-bug had cut its engine immediately above us and there I was in the middle of the road. I looked at the people around me and they stared back, wondering perhaps if I was mad, or certainly fool-hardy. I waited. It was a moment frozen in time. The explosion, when it came, was almost an anti-climax. It took place behind some office buildings, causing barely a shudder. Londoners came out from their office doorways, or picked themselves up and brushed themselves down, looking embarrassed. They started their lives again where they had left them, except of course those who were the victims. I went towards the Station and thought no more about it – until now!

One night I awoke to the sound of a heavy explosion. There had been no air-raid warning, no sound of planes, no Doodle-bugs. We had been told to expect something new, something revolutionary, a true secret weapon, something only the Germans could invent. Lying there in my dark room I thought: "that's it – the new secret weapon".

When we woke up the next morning we read in the newspapers that it was what became known as the V2, a rocket that could be launched from continental Europe to deliver an explosive package many miles away. We did not realise it then, of course, but we were at the beginning of a new age, a lethal step on the road to man's exploration of what he calls space, of a landing on the moon, of satellites circulating the earth

Looking back now an even more terrible thought occurs. The rocket itself did not have a significant impact on the course of the war, but supposing it had been carrying a new and even more terrible warhead, the invention of which was not so very far in the future and possibly capable of development by those same scientists responsible for rocket technology. That would have reduced Great Britain to a devastated land with a subject people and the rest of the world a foil to evil regimes. Fortunately the USA got it first. So closely does destiny roll the dice.

Chapter 5 – Dangerous daylight

One ironic outcome from the onset of war was that my family became, if not prosperous, certainly one step out of the more dismal depths of poverty. Too old to be a combatant, my father lifted himself from the armchair in which he had vegetated for so long and participated in what was known as the ARP (Air Raid Precautions) and CD (Civil Defence), for which he received a modest stipend from the State.

Those involved donned arm bands and "tin helmets" and patrolled the streets ensuring that the black-out regulations were not contravened. No chink of light should be seen from a window, car head-lights were obscured except for a tiny purple square (even cigarettes had to be shielded). They assisted in the emergency services in the event of an air-raid and my father served in 24-hour shifts as a stretcher-bearer at a school in White Hart Lane.

Sometimes, after a night of bombing, he would come home, silent and subdued. No doubt it reminded him of his experiences in Flanders, of stretchers carrying the mutilated bodies of soldiers to their last resting place. He seemed to derive some measure of solace from the miseries of his life by the cultivation of an allotment, a practice the government encouraged to support the provision of food during the stringent years of rationing. It was located a couple of miles away and eventually he added a second, the same distance in the opposite direction.

I was required to assist and pushed a rickety, home-made wheel-barrow to and fro laden with potatoes, carrots, cos lettuces, huge cabbages and other products of our toil. I recall the rigours of the horticultural work, the digging, the hoeing, but there was also satisfaction in harvesting the green beans, the peas, the tomatoes and lifting a fork from the soil to find a clutch of potatoes I had planted as seeds - the right way up, of course!

My mother enjoyed an even more startling transformation. She discovered a latent skill in rudimentary accountancy. Because of the shortage of male staff, she was able to find work at cash tills in such chain store provision suppliers as Home and Colonial and Williams Brothers. Eventually she even became a cashier behind the counter of the local Post Office.

My brother Eric volunteered for the Merchant Navy and disappeared across the Atlantic to return periodically with stories of the terrors that befell the convoys in the Western Approaches. He served on oil tankers and related how he would sit on the rail of the ship, watching as other vessels were blown-up and waiting for his turn. He came home laden with glamorous trophies such as Lucky Strike and Camel cigarettes and Arrow shirts with "Trubenized" collars. I longed to follow him, to find myself in that magical world of the sea described in books like Coral Island and Treasure Island.

My older brother Fred evinced signs that the epilepsy that had troubled him as a teenager had returned and he was, in fact, harbouring something considerably more complex. His marriage broke up. He left his attractive wife and fine flat and came to live with us. I knew that he had suffered "fits", which my mother put down to his spending a holiday in a caravan with no proper pillows on the bed so that his head was lower than his body - such was the level of popular medical knowledge in those days! She could not apply this diagnosis to his present behaviour, however. Words like schizophrenia and dementia, if they existed then, were unknown to us. Strangely, his delusions did not seem to affect his piano playing, which to my ears at least remained expressive.

As the air raids became more frequent and intense, children at school were given the option of taking cover in a school shelter during a raid, or returning home. My mother insisted that I should return home when the siren went. It was part of her curious philosophy that we should stay – or go – together, but ironically both she and my father would be away on their various duties, so they were not present anyway. I had to walk the half a mile or so home through the attacks. Fortunately no bombs fell near me, but I remember the pinging sound of the shrapnel from the anti-aircraft fire. We children used to collect these pieces of jagged metal as souvenirs.

Arrived home, I would find only Fred there, usually playing the piano. I would sit and listen. He had grown a dark beard and looked gaunt. Occasionally, he would stop and examine the palms of his hands. When I asked him why, he simply gazed at me as if pityingly. I gathered later that he was looking for evidence of the stigmata. It was the Moonlight Sonata, with Anton Walbrook playing as the bombs dropped on Warsaw. But this was no phantasy of the "silver screen". This was real and I was living it. I often think of my brother's sad life during those dark days, fuelled by prejudice and ignorance. The astonishing thing is that eventually he came through it. His was a story that showed how there is hope in even the most unlikely prognosis.

So I entered my teen age years with the world deeply involved in war. Looking back, however, it seems that life was in many ways better for us than it is for today's youth. None of us had cars, but we had a surprising degree of mobility, either by public transport or bicycle, which all of us owned. There was also a great deal to occupy ourselves with. Friday night was youth club night, housed in what was called Walker Hall, although we never knew why. There, we would play table tennis or dance to records (78s) played on a gramophone. On one occasion we put on a play. It was a one-act comedy called "Queer Street", all about an habitual criminal whose daughter's boy-friend was a policeman. I played the father - my second public appearance on the stage.

I even acquired a part-time job at a "gentlemen's outfitters" in Wood Green High Street. The elderly owner was not conscripted into national service, but he had no assistants. and he particularly needed help on what were usually busy Saturdays. So he employed me for that day. It was a fascinating experience at a time when men of all classes and ages chose their clothes with some care, having due regard to quality of material, cut, and, of course, price.

Blue jeans were worn only for "manual" work and what became known as the t-shirt was never seen in polite society! The crease down the front of men's trousers was preserved in a "trousers press" and required pressing occasionally. The better quality ones were of worsted, those cheaper, gabardine. "Turnups" were *de rigueur*. Indeed, during the war because of the shortage of cloth they were illegal. To circumvent this we would sell trousers a couple of inches longer in the leg, so that they could be ironed and stitched into place. I was very disconcerted when I was shown for the first time how the "inside leg" measurement was obtained by running a tape measure from a customer's ankle up to his groin, something however, to which I had to accustom myself!

Trousers were looser than they are today, particularly in the waist, so that they were held up with braces. These were called suspenders in the USA, which in this country was the word used for devices that held up socks. One of the purposes of waistcoats, of course, was to conceal the braces. They also provided a plethora of pockets to hold such things as watches (usually attached to chains) and pens.

Shirts had soft collars, until the "Trubenized" method was imported from the States. Before that they were stiffened by the insertion of little plastic strips. For smart wear one wore a collarless shirt to which a white one, possibly stiffened with starch, could be attached with studs Ties were essential wear - as indeed they still are in some circumstances. They were always tied in the same way until one day the Duke of Windsor appeared in public wearing one with a new triangular knot with a cut-away collar. Known as the Windsor knot, It became all the rage and is, of course, still popular today.

Shirt cuffs were often turned back, stiffened with starch and fastened with cuff-links. Underwear was usually in "flannelette" with the pants very modest in design. Vests were identical to those one wears today. Shoes were usually lace-ups, little different from those currently worn except that both soles (rubber) and heels (leather) could be replaced at a cobblers when worn down.

Men wore hats, of course, occasionally the top hat, but usually the bowler, which had to be brushed and cared for. Then the trilby became fashionable, particularly for the younger generation. They came in many shapes and styles, worn formally straight on the head, or more rakishly in emulation of famous film stars. The so-called "working man" favoured the flat cap. "Baseball" caps had yet to make their appearance.

Young men always dressed with care when going out, even to the cinema or cycling to meet friends. We used cycle clips to protect trouser legs from oily chains. It is surprising perhaps that men's fashions (unlike women's) have changed so little throughout the decades. The "sports jacket" (often tweed) and the "blazer" (single- or double-breasted) are still worn. Seventy years later I still have examples of both in my wardrobe and, believe it or not, a pair of trousers with turn-ups, which is astonishing, because it was an absurd practice, serving no purpose except to gather fluff, dirt and even cigarette ends!

There always seemed to be something with which to occupy ourselves. Principal source of entertainment was, of course, the cinema, with some half a dozen within easy reach. Then there were dance halls in Southgate, Harringay and Tottenham. On rare occasions one of the "big bands" would visit and play concerts in a cinema to enthusiastic audiences of a few hundreds, contrasting with the modern pop concerts attended by tens of thousands! I did not go regularly to church on Sunday and, after lunch would meet with friends in one of the nearby parks, or cycle to Hadley Wood and even more distant Epping Forest.

At 14 I began attendance at Tottenham Technical College – Commercial Section. For those in the Industrial Section the course was for three years and interestingly for boys only, whereas mine lasted only two years. It was of mixed gender, and obviously intended to train the secretaries of the future, so that girls outnumbered boys by a considerable margin. There was a heavy emphasis on typewriting and Pitman's shorthand, but the inclusion of book-keeping, however, suggests that boys were going to be encouraged to choose accountancy as a career.

The educational concept of a technical college as a kind of apprenticeship seemed basically sound, but there were a number of short-comings so far as the commercial section was concerned. On the technical side most of the teaching was around benches and in a work-place environment. As potential office workers we were told we were going to learn to be city ladies and gentlemen and were expected as act accordingly. But instead of accommodating us in an office environment, they sat us behind desks, with a teacher and black-board out front. They dressed us in maroon blazers and school caps, which tended to encourage us to behave as – well - school children.

With so many of the country's adult population, male and female, engaged in the war effort of one kind or another those who could be spared to teach tended to be ill-trained for the task of controlling unruly teenagers. Girls comprised three quarters of my class and this had a deleterious effect on at least one of the masters, who treated the distaff side with unctuous paternalism, while his attitude towards the small male section was diametrically opposite. He sometimes scarcely managed to refrain from physically attacking us, whom he obviously regarded as evil incarnate. Which perhaps we were!

It was decided to teach us Spanish, which is interesting, although it has to be remembered that we were at war with most of Europe, then under the domination of the Nazi German forces. It is true Spain was governed by the dictator Franco, who was friendly with Hitler and might have been regarded as hostile, nevertheless Great Britain still had strong ties and much trade with South American countries, in most of which Spanish was spoken.

The trouble was as children we had developed in an educational system that paid little heed to the niceties of grammar and when we were faced with applying them strictly in a foreign language I am afraid our natural tendency to rebel against anything that was not easily absorbed by our ill-conditioned minds led to a very uncomfortable relationship with our unfortunate teacher. His name was Beatty and we called him Bertie – to his face. He was a very sweet man, who did his best with us, but I am afraid we gave him a very bad time. As soon as I left school I signed up for evening classes in French and studied that until my period of national service began, but to this day I regret not having the mastery of at least one language other than English.

Choosing an occupational course rather than the traditional grammar school was not an entire disaster. Some of its advantages have stayed with me all my life. Learning to be a touch typist has not only facilitated my career as a writer, but also provided me with opportunities for work during my theatrical resting periods. The bookkeeping also gave me a groundwork of accountancy as well as improving my general mathematical skills. We were fortunate in having an English mistress who not only had imagination, but also encouraged us to use ours. The special slants on history and geography taught us that life in the past and elsewhere in the world did not necessarily devolve around the English monarchy and the British Empire.

We travelled to school in a trolleybus, which had replaced the tram as one of the factors making up the marvellously efficient network of transport that, even in wartime conditions, served the population of London. We were a rowdy lot crowding on the top deck. Learning of the hooliganism and generally bad behaviour of so-called modern youth, I am tempted to reflect that the situation has not changed very much, although we never engaged in gang attacks, and would not have dreamed of carrying a knife, let alone a gun. And we did have some justification for a certain lack of discipline. We were, after all, engaged in a life and death struggle with a foe who was only a score or so of miles away across the Channel. We were suffering the exigencies of rationing and a fairly restricted life-style. Our parents, brothers and sisters were being killed in battle. And we were being bombed night and day.

One day I was travelling home from school on the top of the trolley-bus. Some students from another school were behaving boisterously near the front of the bus. One of them threw a tomato that narrowly missed me. In anger I picked it up and hurled it back. Unfortunately, it missed my assailant and hit the vehicle's front window. Even more unfortunately it burst and sprayed the remains of the tomato over the light brown suit of a master from the other school who happened to be sitting in the front seat.

He rose majestically to his feet and demanded to know who had thrown it. He received no reply. We were near the end of our journey and he stormed down the aisle threatening death and damnation on all maroon-blazered hooligans. Cunningly, I got to my feet, took out a handkerchief and attempted to clean his soiled waistcoat. He thanked me and to the joy of my schoolmates, said he was glad to find that one boy at least was well-mannered and polite.

The next day at school assembly there was a terrible hush as the Principal announced that the most awful doom awaited us all. The behaviour on the school bus was unacceptable. From that time on students of the two schools would be released into the public domain at different times. More importantly, the master who had been assailed was demanding retribution, even to the extent of taking legal action. He could be mollified, however, and the good name of the school to some extent salvaged, if the boy responsible for throwing the tomato would own up to his misdeed.

Needless to say I felt it was incumbent on me to do the right thing. I did and was called up before the Principal and treated by him to what I can only describe as a demonstration of venom. He made no attempt to investigate the incident and seemed content to place the blame squarely on pupils of his own school, myself in particular. I was never asked for my side of the incident. The injustice of it rankles to this day.

Because I had owned up and because it was near the end of my time at the school he told me I would not be expelled (!). Nevertheless he obviously wanted to visit on me the utmost in dire retribution. I remember his words to this day: "Rocker", he said, "you are the sort of boy who will grow up to be a man who lives by his wits". He went on: "You may not realise it now, but one day you will need to come to me for a reference". And his face contorted into a snarl as he added: "And you won't get it".

Chapter 6 - Girls and boys come out to play

I kissed a girl for the first time when I was about 12. I recorded the event in a little diary, marked with a large X. We had a lodger at the time whose home was in the South of England, but because of wartime necessity was working in the ticket office of Wood Green Station. One day, in front of members of my family he laughed and scoffed at me for my diary entry, which he had obviously found and read. I don't think he was an unkind man. To him it was presumably a mild joke, but I still remember to this day the embarrassment I felt and even pain at his betrayal.

The girl my virgin lips first experienced was named Rosina, although everyone called her Ena. Ours was a sweet and gentle relationship. We went for walks with her dog, held hands and occasionally I put an arm around her waist. That first kiss was followed by one or two more, but by nothing more overtly sexual. One day she found the dog she was supposed to be looking after had stolen and eaten some meat she had recently bought. It was her family's entire ration for a week and she burst into tears. I put an arm round her shoulders and hugged her, learning that one of the duties of the male is to comfort a loved one and breathe words of consolation into her gently scented hair.

My sister Edna and her husband George rented a little house in the Surrey countryside. It was a former wood-cutters cottage called Barns Thorns not far from Effingham Junction Station on what was then the Southern Railway. With about an acre of ground it was located in the heart of a wood and accessible either by a footpath or a drive through the trees. I can remember to this day its first impression on me when I came upon it nestling at the far side of the clearing, plume of smoke almost inevitably rising from its fairy-tale chimney. I cycled there from my home in North London on my rickety old "roadster" bicycle, almost miraculously travelling along what was then the North Circular Road and down the "arterial" A3!

To me as a Londoner who had rarely strayed outside the confines of the city it was paradise. There were apple trees and plum trees so laden with fruit that I made myself sick sitting in their branches and gorging myself. My memories of my sister are of a dark, saturnine young woman, her personality no doubt influenced by her very difficult relationship with our father, but she was always very kind to me, for which I am eternally grateful. She had two daughters, Gillian and Susan, who have remained close and affectionate towards their aging uncle.

Nowadays the tendency is to be increasingly open about sexual proclivities and activities. Children are taught about sex in schools, have access to screens that show erotic and even pornographic images with little regard for the impact on impressionable minds. I grew up in a world that was secretive, repressed, where sex before marriage was taboo and, once married, husbands and wives generally stayed together. Unmarried pregnancy was regarded as a disaster for both mother and child.

Boys generally were interested in girls, although not quite sure what to do about them, as they seemed a somewhat mysterious race of beings. Male homosexuality was punishable by social exclusion and even prison. Female homosexuality was called the silent love and seldom spoken about. Perhaps for these reasons there was never any question of young teenagers "coming out".

Masturbation was a mortal sin and reputed to make the perpetrator go blind, mad, or at the very least suffer from hirsute palms. Boys at public school were reputedly dragged from their beds and thrashed if this type of activity was discovered under cover of their bedclothes. Looking back one wonders what it was in the secret lives of the masters that drove them to such disproportionate behaviour. They described masturbation as "self-abuse", perhaps to distinguish it in their own minds from the abuse they wished to perpetrate on their charges.

Children today are influenced by the images they see on their television sets or games consoles. In our day it was the heroes and heroines who inhabited the cinema screen and were pictured in the movie magazines and the press generally that motivated our lives. Classification meant that younger children were unable to see films not regarded as conducive to their moral welfare. Nowadays they may switch on the television, or their computer screens, and see images and acts that would at one time have landed those responsible in prison. We saw cowboy heroes shooting evil Indians. Gangsters played by actors like George Raft, Paul Muni, or James Cagney eventually got their just desserts. Now children are able to manipulate the fate of the lawless creatures who kill so remorselessly in their games.

We were spectators of an unreal and strangely sexless world, dreamt up by the writers of the screen-plays and perpetuated by studio publicists. While we watched and fell in love with Judy Garland as a pretty girl skipping along the yellow brick road, we were unaware of the torment behind her unreal and unnatural working life. Until Burt Lancaster and Deborah Kerr rolled in the surf the strongest manifestation of sexual attraction was the kiss that provided the closing shot of many a Hollywood film. So the average young male dreamed of achieving a similar exotic juxtaposition. We knew sex existed, but felt unable to participate in it without running the risk of being ostracized socially and perhaps suffering eternal damnation.

So far as I was concerned, as adolescence tightened its grip the need to become associated with someone of the opposite sex intensified. I was painfully thin and lacked the masculine characteristics that were traditionally regarded as desirable in a man. Other boys seemed able to achieve impressive sun tans. I remained as pale as the vanilla ice-cream we consumed so hungrily. I saw myself as the personification of the weak male creature who suffered having sand kicked in his face on the beach by those who were better endowed.

I was a poor swimmer. I did obtain a certificate for swimming 250 yards, but I could manage only a breast stroke. My compatriots swam with the powerful Australian crawl, or what was for me an even more unachievable back stroke. I could not bring myself to dive, or even jump in from the side of a swimming pool, while they would hurl themselves off the top of the high diving board in spectacularly mock or real dives.

However, as I watched the male film stars of the day achieve their romantic successes on the cinema screen, I began to realise that women are often attracted by the most unlikely physical specimens. They could be lanky and physically unimpressive like Henry Fonda and James Stewart, or short and downright ugly like James Cagney and Edward G. Robinson. Fred Astaire and Bing Crosby could sing or dance, but they were not exactly robust physical specimens. I decided to put these observations to the test.

I was 15 years of age and in the second year of the commercial college. There was a girl in the earlier class, whose name was Iris. She wore high-heeled shoes and dresses with hems that stopped short above the knees – frowned upon in those days. She also filled out the top half of her frocks in an interesting way. My fellow male schoolmates saw her as a sex object and made scatological remarks about her behind closed fists.

Despite my unprepossessing appearance I was not lacking in moral courage, so one day, with a boldness that seems surprising to me even now, I went up to the front door of her house in Enfield, knocked, and invited her out. She accepted and to my astonishment I found myself dating the most desirable girl in the college. One day I asked my pretty little paramour how it was that she seemed to prefer the company of a wimp like me, rather than those glamorous exponents of physical dexterity and attractiveness who disported themselves to such advantage at the swimming pools. "Oh! Those!" I remember she responded. "We girls don't think much of those show-offs."

Our relationship developed until we actually became engaged to be married. I bought her a ring, which she wore proudly, defying her father's demand to "get that thing off". He was inclined to be strict with her, because she was an only child and no doubt he sensed the latent sexuality that could lead to what would then have been described as "trouble". He would bemoan the possibility that she would have "a couple of kids around her skirts before she was 20". In fact, she did, although it was none of my doing.

She obviously had a very powerful maternal instinct, which I was too immature to appreciate or satisfy. We were quite passionate in our embraces, kissing and cuddling and occasionally my fingers would wander near the secret chasm of her sexuality, but something in the pressures of my upbringing, linked to the social mores of the day, prevented me from going "all the way".

Her biological clock, however, was ticking to a different time scale from mine. She felt the lure of "metal more attractive" and she found it in one of the fairgrounds that were a magnet for us youngsters then, perhaps because of the bright lights and the romance surrounding their transient nature, their reputedly illicit dealings. They were a useful source of employment for young men deserting from the army and it was with one of these that Iris formed a liaison. At first I did not consider him a potential rival, even when my fiancée reported that in the course of conversation he had told her he was not interested in "kid's stuff".

Later I will be recalling the outcome of this tale, which has echoes of what later achieved fame on stage and screen as the musical "Carousel".

Chapter 7 – A troubling conflict

Meanwhile the injustice of my headmaster attempting to ruin my career culminated in something of a triumph for me. It seemed generally accepted by my fellow students that I did not stand a hope of finding gainful employment, but I was rescued from this awful fate by the intervention of my brother Fred, who was enjoying something of a remission from his debilitating condition. At some time in his life he had worked as a porter on a local railway station, where he had made the acquaintance of a man who was in a responsible executive position as secretary of a professional institution. Due to the shortage of labour in the war this person had been without assistance for some time and was looking for someone with my particular skills. My brother recommended me to him and a meeting was arranged at his office off Victoria Street, Central London.

I could type, write shorthand, had the rudiments of bookkeeping and was prepared to make up for any deficiencies I might have in grammar. The question of my unsatisfactory school record was raised, but he was prepared to take a chance on me and did so, with the result that I was one of the first from my class to leave and start work. My new boss did not even bother to ask for a reference. Later, I was to realise why.

My work included taking dictation in Pitman's shorthand and typing on what was, of course, a manual typewriter. It was my first involvement in association management, work that I was to return to 50 years later. I even experienced my first Annual General Meeting, which took place, if I recall, at the Waldorf Hotel, in the Aldwych, London. I sat on the top table next to the secretary, who introduced me to members as the Institution's new staff, for which I received a small round of applause.

My employer, who was the only other occupant in the

office, seemed a kindly man and took a keen interest in my well-being. For example, he introduced me to, and paid for, a course in English grammar, which I embraced with enthusiasm, and also encouraged me to attend evening classes in French. Sadly the motive for this kindness and care became apparent as he began to demonstrate a more personal interest in me, which, as it became increasingly sexual, I found unpleasant, offensive and deeply troubling. A situation that had been so greatly to my advantage now turned out to have its bitter side and for the first time I was experiencing not only the perfidy of human nature, but also the irony of fate.

What happened never amounted to serious abuse and my reaction to it was mostly embarrassment. I was careful not to give him any encouragement. There was nothing I could do about it. The whole aspect of sexual abuse is one that has received much publicity in modern times, but even now, it seems, young victims find it difficult to escape from the situation. In my case there was no one to whom I could complain, or seek advice. Who would have believed me? He was a highly respected member of society. I had left school under a cloud and would be regarded as your typical rebellious young adult. I would not only be misbelieved, but might have been vilified and accused of malicious motives. I was the typical vulnerable youngster being taken advantage of by someone in authority.

I think he honestly believed what he was doing reflected some kind of love on his part. When I visited him while on leave from the Merchant Navy I mentioned that I had read Shakespeare's sonnets and he wondered whether this had given me a greater understanding of what had transpired. It had not! I cannot bring myself to hate him for what he did, or attempted to do. He had a grown-up daughter, but no sons, and his was probably a lonely life in his little office and his home in Surrey. Fortunately I was strong enough physically to resist his approaches and mentally secure in my own sexuality so I am happy to say I did not suffer from the kind of mental conflict such predatory behaviour can arouse in young men.

His behaviour was partly mitigated by his help in another way. World War II being at its height, all young men were conscripted by the time they were seventeen and a half. A new and, to me, alarming element entered into this process. There was concern in government that the absence of younger men serving overseas was leading to a serious depletion in the manpower available to run industry at home. Indeed, historians have suggested that a similar situation in Nazi Germany contributed to its downfall.

The Minister of Labour at the time, Ernest Bevin, introduced the idea of selecting some young men by ballot to work in the mines. They became known as Bevin boys and the prospect of working as a miner was of greater dread to teenagers than having to join the army, particularly those who lived in the south of England for whom mining constituted an alien activity in what to Londoners were almost foreign countries.

As a seaman my brother was experiencing the threat of sailing in the convoys attacked by the German U-boats in the terrible "Western Approaches. The dangers he encountered seemed to pale against the prospect of a life down the mines. So well before my conscription papers were due to arrive, I volunteered to join the Merchant Navy. In order to be accepted, however, I had to spend time at what was known as a sea school.

One of these was Gravesend Sea School, based on a hulk known as the Vindicatrix. This had been anchored on the River Thames until towed as a war-time evacuation measure to a location in Sharpness Docks, near Bristol. The physical requirements for intending "students" were not stringent, but did require a chest measurement of at least 32 inches. Having suffered from the stringencies of pre-war and war-time diets, mine was only 28½! I had to increase my girth by three and a half inches in six months. I started on a course of exercise, including swimming

I also needed a reference not only from my employer,

but also from the College, which the principal had vowed he would never give me. My employer wrote and told him that his view of me had not been borne out by his experience and strongly recommended that he should change his view. To my relief and great satisfaction I enjoyed the further triumph of getting the reference.

There was one further requirement. In order to be accepted at the school there had to be a guarantee that I would be offered a job on a ship at the end of training. My employer was acquainted with someone who was on the board of a shipping company. I was sent to visit him at his nearby office and after the interview was granted the necessary assurance.

My second application to the training school was accepted. On the night before I set out on the great adventure my girl-friend Iris spent the night in a spare bedroom in our house. After my parents had gone to bed I climbed in beside her for a cuddle and fondle. Then we both fell asleep to be woken in the morning by my horrified parents, whose main concern was that we had not "gone all the way", which we had not. Nevertheless it was an embarrassing moment and taught me an important lesson for the future: that when one sleeps with a person one is not supposed to be sleeping with one should make a point of not going to sleep.

Chapter 8 - Upon a painted ocean

For the first three weeks we slept not on board the Vindicatrix, but in a shore-based barracks, where conditions were probably not much different from those endured in the army. When we got on to the hulk, however, things were rather more primitive. It was January, a bitterly cold mid-winter, in a gaunt forbidding landscape. We were woken at 6.0 am, herded on to the open upper deck in bare feet and our underwear to wash in cold water drawn into a bucket from a stand pipe. I cannot remember showering all the time I was on board. Food was almost inedible. Officers, or warders as we described them, walked about swinging rubber truncheons, which they would not hesitate to use. We were told that the object of the stringent conditions was to prepare us for life at sea, but I never found on even the smallest, dirtiest rust-bucket of a tanker anything that resembled what we endured at Sharpness.

On the recommendation of my brother and to follow in his footsteps, I had opted to join the catering staff so that my period of training was half the length of the 12 weeks undertaken by those who were going to become deckhands. Instead of being taught how to tie knots and scrape metalwork, we learnt the art of placing knives and forks on the table, doling out baked beans on to plates, making up bunks and scrubbing the cabin decks. For some reason we were dressed in strange blue striped jackets, which I never saw worn anywhere at sea.

Eventually, the ordeal came to an end and I found myself making my way to join my first ship. This was one of three cargo-passenger liners of similar design recently introduced to service by Houlder Brothers. She was quite advanced in design with accommodation for both passengers and crew located aft. Mid-ships and the fore part of the ship were taken up by the refrigerated cargo holds, which gave it a racy, speedy look. Twelve first class cabins carried 24 passengers, one of whom on our outward journey was to be Sir Montague Eddie, a British statesman who, we learnt, was bound to South America in order to negotiate the sale of the British railway system to the Argentine government.

The ship was berthed at Canada Dock in Liverpool, and I travelled to it on the overhead railway, which carried dock workers and merchant seamen past all the docks in that busy port. It was built up on metal girders that years later were found to be severely corroded, resulting in the line's closure.

I arrived at 8.0 pm and reported to the chief steward/purser, who seemed a kind man. I thought it odd, however, when he suggested that in order to recover from my journey I should get undressed and climb into my bunk where he would bring me a cup of tea, which he did! It was certainly very different from my experience on the Vindicatrix.

The next day I met three sprightly assistant stewards in their 20s. They had served on the route for some time, waiting on tables and looking after the passengers generally, doing well out of the tips they earned. There was also a "second" steward, whose main job apart from ensuring that we did our jobs effectively, was to serve in the bar and keep it spruce and tidy.

My official title was" cabin boy" and I would be responsible for the most menial tasks in the department. There was also a "galley boy" most of whose time seemed to be taken up by peeling potatoes! Passengers received first-class cuisine, at breakfast, lunch, afternoon tea and dinner, cooked by a master chef and two assistant cooks, one of whom was the baker

Needless to say I couldn't wait for the ship to sail and my big adventure to begin. As a boy I had been fascinated by the sea, although I only knew about it from my reading and occasional visits to the seaside. One of my favourite books was Coral Island, which I had read over and over. We sailed at last, but my encounter with the great ocean was to be delayed a little longer. The ship had been subjected to major repairs in dock but soon after we left Liverpool she developed some kind of trouble with the engine and anchored off Milford Haven. While we were wallowing there we received news that caused great excitement. The war in Europe was over. This was VE day. We stood around a radio in a public area and heard a description of the celebrations in Britain. They were dancing the conga in the Strand and cheering the royal family in the Mall. The announcer told us: "London is the place to be today". London! My home. A city where I had spent five years of war, enduring the bombs and the blackout, the rationing and the privations.

The whole of England was celebrating, but we weren't allowed to. We were still within the three-mile limit so the bond could not be opened, and the captain was also presumably not prepared to risk having a drunken crew on his hands. The passengers were, however, already on board and could celebrate from bar stock, which we had to serve them. They also had to be fed so that while people in England were tearing down the black-out curtains and removing their bedding from air-raid shelters, I personally had to wash up a mountain of china, glassware and silver cutlery, not to mention the vast array of metal cooking utensils, pots, pans and serving dishes.

Within a day or two, however, we sailed for South America and at last I was rocked in one of mother earth's great oceanic cradles. When we put out into the North Atlantic I loved the swirl and sway of the vessel as I walked along the decks, holding on to the rails. I took any opportunity I could to look out of the big windows of the high forward saloon and watch the waves breaking over the cargo holds as the bows of the handsome ship plunged into the sea.

I had thought that the flying fish described in Coral Island were a figment of the author's imagination, but there they were, skipping out of the water from swell to swell as the ship hit their schools. There were porpoises, too - or were they dolphins? - sporting with the great monster in their midst, falling back on to its bows so that they could be pushed along. Older members of the crew jeered at my youthful enthusiasm and tried very hard to make me seasick, with descriptions of fatty pork being lowered down the throat and other fanciful devices! But I would have none of it.

Actual life on board the ship itself, however, was very different from the poetic images I had read in books or the excitement of the sea itself. I worked a 12-hour day, spread over 14 hours with a two hours rest period in the afternoon. My first job at six am was to scrub alleyway decks. Then I prepared the "sink" for breakfast dishwashing. Despite the fact that I was on board a modern, state-of-the-art ocean liner conditions in the "pantry" were primitive to say the least. I filled the sink with cold water, which was heated with steam pipes. Detergent was provided by hard soap in a perforated tin that was shaken by hand in the water. The silver cutlery used in the saloon had to be treated with special care to avoid damage. Food was brought in from the galley to be placed in large hot-presses and dispensed to the stewards entering from the saloon. The worst part of my job was cleaning the grease from the heavy metal trays.

My main morning task was to clean the passengers' bathrooms and toilets. If I was able to finish this early I would usually hide myself away somewhere as the second steward would come looking for me to help him clean and tidy up his bar. If he failed to find me he would report me to the Chief Steward as the lazy good-for-nothing I probably was! Lunch was quite a substantial meal for the passengers, comprising dishes like shepherds' pie, curries, etc, which meant a great deal more washing up for me.

Clearing up after lunch took me till two pm, my first break and an opportunity to eat. Then I would rest, sometimes in a chair out on deck, quite a luxury for an earth-bound English boy who had never known exotic sun and a warm wind blowing over the waves. Tea was served at 4.0 pm, so I was back to work coping with the silver service. That left little time before it was necessary to prepare for dinner, which had seven courses if one included the preliminary canapés and cocktails and the following cheese and biscuits and port. As the assistant stewards were setting up in the saloon before the passengers arrived I was given the opportunity to watch and learn how the rich liked their tables prepared.

Sometimes when finishing the washing up on my own in the pantry I would be visited by the galley boy, who weighed 18 stone and had decided that my 8 ½ stone was fair game on which to exercise his pugilistic skills. I decided I had a better chance of surviving if I faced the challenge and gave as good as I got. We wrestled, but I was obviously unable to overcome his weight advantage and we usually finished up on the greasy floor with his heavy weight subduing my supine body. Then, presumably having established his superiority, he would let me up. Neither of us suffered any mishap, and eventually he tired of the sport. So did I!

From this I learnt how important it was to stand up for myself. Thin and underweight, I would have been an obvious target for bullying, but once my fellow crew members learnt that I was not an easy victim they left me alone, or engaged in playful encounters that I responded to in good part. There was one occasion that I remember with some pride. I was sunning myself with other members of the catering staff on the fore-deck of the ship. There were one or two female passengers sun-bathing nearby and one of the stewards, a tall blonde, bronzed Irishman called O'Leary decided to show off to them by inflicting a little arm twisting and leg-bending on me. I have always had something of an instinct for the martial arts I later indulged in as a sport and my experiences with the galley boy also stood me in good stead. I soon had him stumbling all over the deck. He began to look foolish and became increasingly frustrated and annoyed. The encounter looked as if it would turn serious until other members of the catering staff stepped in and stopped it.

There was, however, another form of bullying on board that was more difficult to deal with, something that nowadays would be recognised as abuse. I was no longer a child, of course, being by this time 17, but I was entirely subservient to the Chief Steward, who became determined to take advantage of his authoritative position. Obviously, his kindness in tucking me up in bed with a cup of tea when I arrived on board had a sinister motive. Quite early on in the voyage he began to make his sexual intentions towards me obvious. Fortunately my experiences in the London office had prepared me for the situation and I made it clear that his advances were unwelcome and would be repulsed, violently if necessary. He did not take his rejection kindly. One day he confronted me when I was cleaning a passenger's bathroom. I resisted his advances. He was a plump, out-of-condition middle-aged man. I was young, fit, strong and, more importantly fleeter of foot. He chased me around the cabins, like a scene from a Carry On film, but I made sure he did not catch me.

I can still see him now in his uniform shorts, his pale, fleshy knees trembling as he sat talking to the other members of the catering staff. They were respectful towards him, if only because their jobs did to some extent depend on him, but fortunately for my situation they were all heterosexual, discussing with eager anticipation the paradise lying ahead in Buenos Aires. The Chief Steward poured scorn on their enthusiasm for women, denigrating their dalliance with the "nasty dirty girls". He expressed himself unable to understand why men wanted to gaze at naked women in strip clubs trying, as he pointed out, to see something that did not exist! He preferred to spend his time on board and no doubt hoped that I would too, but in that he was disappointed

Before BA the ship put in at Montevideo, Uruguay, my first foreign port. I was working below when we docked and we were alongside before I was able to get on deck. When I did I was greeted with a sight that took my breath away. The whole of my teen-age years had been spent in the dark of a blacked-out city. My only experience of dockland was an occasional visit to the bombed port of London and the few weeks I had spent in grimy Liverpool. What I beheld when I went up on deck and first set eyes on Montevideo was a wonderland of light and colour. The sun was setting with an orange glow, reflected on the olive green water of the River Plate - La Plata. In contrast to the dirty grey of Liverpool, the pink and white dock buildings were lit in the twilight by pleasantly designed street lamps.

Many of the passengers went visiting ashore so there was less for us to do in the evening. We were, course, civilians and not bound by naval discipline, so were free to follow them once our daily tasks were over. There, my sense of wonder increased. There was a smell in the air that was a mixture of strong cigars and even stronger perfume. The music emanating from the bars and restaurants were those Latin rhythms that had been made so popular in Hollywood movies. Perhaps it was my fancy but people seemed to walk with a dance in their step. We wandered along the colourful, well-lit streets, drank sweet vermouth in the open-air cafes and enjoyed food that I had never experienced, huge beef steaks and exotic desserts.

We went to a night club where there were music and dancing and more beautiful young women than I have ever seen gathered in one place at one time. As we sat drinking one of them came up to me and asked me to dance. South American music had already found its way into the dance halls of the UK so I did not disgrace myself. My pretty little partner seemed delighted with me and told me her name was Musetta, but it all came to an end when she asked me if I had *"dinero"*. We had been warned about this when we had been issued with our meagre allowance before coming ashore, so I had to say I had no money. She shook her head sadly and said: "But we can still dance". And we did.

After a few days the ship was moved across the river to Buenos Aires, passing on its way the remains of the Graf

Spee, relic of a famous sea battle, protruding from the water. BA was even more imposing than Monte, with its tall buildings, grid-pattern New York style streets and little *Collectivo* buses that linked the docks of Boca and Retiro through the centre of the city.

My companions would stay ashore all night, visiting one of the dance clubs to select partners before taking them to El Tigre, a hotel offering appropriate accommodation. The ship's butcher (*el carnicero*) had a different approach. He had a wife in England and for many years had maintained a second partner in Buenos Aires apparently dividing his attentions faithfully between them. Perhaps still influenced by cinema romance, I was content to soak up the huge excitement of the exotic city and resist the lure of experiences that would conflict with my sense of fidelity to a young lady I had left in England.

Eventually, the holds of the ship were full of meat and we set out again across the Atlantic, destined however not to Britain, but to other countries in Europe still recovering from the exigencies of war. We delivered meat to Gibraltar; to the south Italian port of Taranto, where we saw *Il Duce's* scuttled navy; and then to devastated Malta, which had suffered years of bombardment and near starvation, refusing to surrender to the Nazi threat.

We anchored in the magnificent Grand Harbour to unload the first cargo of meat to arrive on that beleaguered island since the end of hostilities. My memory is of a land where scarcely any buildings remained undamaged, many completely flattened by both air and sea bombardment. The sense of devastation was relieved only by the hospitality and indomitable spirit of the Maltese people. I caught a little bus to a local seaside resort, where I bathed my feet in the warm waters of the Mediterranean and thought of the contrast between the beauty of my surroundings and the horrors of the war that had been visited on this tiny community.

Then back to South America again: Montevideo, Buenos Aires and Rosario, a port further up the River

Plate, about which, however, I have no recollection at all. Once reloaded with meat, the ship sailed for England. A few days before we docked the Chief Steward called me into his office and told me I had not given satisfactory service during my time on board. Without his recommendation I would not be offered work with the company again. I had, he said, a few days in which to redeem myself. It was blackmail, but his hand was a weak one, both literally and metaphorically. I was not concerned about a future career in either the company or the merchant navy. There would be other ships and, anyway, at the end of three years my period of service would be over. Many years later my professional career as a magazine editor led me to meet with an executive from that shipping company. I told him about my experience and the activities of the Chief Steward. He shook his head sadly. "Yes", he said, "We had our doubts about him".

We docked this time in the Thames to be hailed by London's *Evening News* as the first ship after the War to bring back a cargo of meat from the Argentine. As soon as I could I went out to Enfield and called on Iris. To my surprise I was greeted by her parents more warmly than had been my experience in the past. The reason soon became apparent. She had been seeing rather too much of her friend from the fair ground and I was obviously a more desirable boyfriend.

So with their encouragement we saw one another nearly every day and our relationship developed. Life was really quite idyllic. In addition to being pretty and sexy, she was an intelligent girl. Leaving the commercial college she had obtained a job as secretary to neuro-surgeons at Chase Farm Hospital, near her home in Enfield. This apparently involved attending operations and taking notes, work she should not strictly have been doing under the age of 18. But this was a time of staff shortages, when bureaucratic considerations were not always followed. One of the surgeons she worked for was named Northfield; the other, appropriately enough, Brain; both of them became celebrated in later years.

The hospital was shared by injured patients from the US air force, tall, colourful officers, many of them pilots, carrying with them a kind of Hollywood glamour. Some had also adopted, perhaps from the films, novel attitudes towards discipline. One of them was nick-named "Hyser", because he would greet a superior officer with a wave of the hand and the salutation "Hi sir". They were delightful, friendly young men and so far as I know there was never any conflict between the two strangely contrasting aspects of the medical facility.

There appeared to be no restrictions on the length of time a merchant seaman could remain on leave. Houlder Brothers did not approach me to re-join their ships, so I had no job to go to. My only concern was that officialdom might catch up with me resulting in army service, or worse still, coal mining.

When I had been home for about three weeks my brother, Eric, came home from one of his trips. There was, he said, a vacancy for a pantry boy on board his ship, a tanker docked in London. It would be sailing shortly, destination presumably the Caribbean and possibly even the States. Did I want the job? At first, I demurred. I was reluctant to leave Iris. He asked me if I wanted to risk conscription for the sake of a girl. He himself was engaged to be married but was quite prepared to put the ceremony off until after another trip if I would join him. He obviously thought it would be pleasant for us to be sailing together and perhaps enjoy good times ashore in foreign ports.

So I agreed and turned my back on my love affair, not realising that it was for the last time. The ship was the mv Northia, a Shell company tanker presumably built to serve that company's refineries in the ports around the Caribbean. Sadly, however, when we set sail we found that we would be travelling not to the glamorous West Indies, but to the heat and sand of the Middle East. We were bound for what was then called the Persian Gulf. This was dreaded by all who served on the little 15,000-ton oil tankers of those days, to such an extent that, if asked, any would say they preferred the dangers of the U-boats and Atlantic storms, to what was known as the Abadan run.

Eric's expectation had been that we would only be serving in a short trip to the Americas and back so that his wedding would not be too long delayed. I also did not want to be parted from Iris for more than a few weeks. The reality was that once an oil tanker had passed through the Suez Canal the company would want to delay its return as long as possible to avoid the charges involved. It would stay out there, picking up oil in the Gulf and delivering it to ports further east Officially merchant seamen were bound by two-yearly articles, which they could terminate prematurely only if the ship returned to a port in the UK. Fortunately, although crews might be expected to be away from home for two years, at the end of one the ship would need to return to the UK for a rest and a refit!

Chapter 9 - Down to the sea in a hulk

Life on board the MV Northia was very different from my first ship. I still worked a gruelling 12 hour day, but instead of a luxury liner gliding majestically over the ocean I was now sailing on a tiny oil tank, which allowed itself to be bucketed and buffeted by even the least of waves and winds. The lower ranks of the crew lived in accommodation aft, among the motors, the galley and the refrigerated storerooms. The officers' cabins and saloon were located amidships, reached along a companionway traversing a well-deck under which were the cargo tanks.

Apart from two cooks and a "galley boy" the catering department comprised: the Chief Steward, a large fat man named Louis; a small, lean Second Steward, who looked after the catering stores, particularly the alcohol in the "bond"; my brother and one other Assistant Steward, who looked after the officers, serving their meals and keeping their accommodation clean and tidy My official title was still Pantry Boy, but I was also known as the "bosun's peggy" and I had to look after the boatswain and other Petty Officers, for whom I served meals in their mess and cleaned their cabins.

The bosun was in charge of the crew at what would, in a military context, have been sergeant major level. The other petty officers were the electrician (sparks); storekeeper, whose name identifies his work; pump-man, who had responsibility for the ship's cargo of oil; and a "donkey-man", whose job was to maintain all the various pieces of oil-fuelled apparatus on board. I remember him as a man who never seemed free from the oil that coated his clothes, his hands, his arms and even his face despite the frequent application of an oily rag.

There was also a carpenter (chips), who, in addition to his usual duties, kept the key to the tap accessing the cold water in the refrigerator. During the hot weather it was rationed as a thirsty crew would have drunk it dry in hours.

They blamed him for denying access, although he did so under orders. This made him extremely unpopular and he inevitably became the butt of bullying by the crew, suffering sometimes physical violence. Curiously a similar fate befell the carpenter in the second of the two tankers on which I served.

We left England in November, sailing down a Channel full of squalls that blew rain and sea spray in our faces. The weather became even worse in the Bay of Biscay, but when we passed through the Straits of Gibraltar into the Mediterranean, it was like Dorothy opening the door into the Technicolour land of Oz. We threw off the long trousers and heavy sweaters and donned the tropical clothes we were destined to wear for many a long month, although there would come a time when we would hate the heat and the sun and long for the invigoration of cool wind and rain.

Passing through the Suez Canal was an unreal experience. The ship moved silently and large through low banks of spreading desert or high walls of strange rock formations. Occasionally we caught glimpses of camel riders, who would pause in their peregrinations to gaze at this modern monster invading their ancient land. We spent Christmas in the Red Sea and celebrated with a bottle of gin unexpectedly supplied by the Chief Steward. Perhaps he had a presentiment of what was to come. He was anxious about his health and had been warned that his obesity presented a particular danger in the hot weather.

We had heard of the terrible heat we were to expect in the Gulf, but when we arrived in January at our first port, Abadan, we found it was no worse than an English heatwave. We could not imagine any harm coming from this gloriously benign weather. The old hands shook their heads and warned us that, if we were still visiting the place in August we would find it greatly different. They told us terrible stories of what lay ahead, how the heat in the Gulf could dry up the body like an old withered orange, tough metal would buckle and warp, men would go mad. With the tropical sun on our shoulders and nights sweet for sleeping we did not believe them, or if we believed did not care.

Sadly when we arrived in Abadan I received what was then known to all in the services as a "Dear John letter". Iris no longer wished to be engaged to me. The relationship with the young fair-ground worker had developed. Indeed, when I arrived home a year later she already had a child by this young man and shortly after conceived another, confirming that teenage pregnancy is by no means a unique feature of the present day. This was sad for me but the romance had a happy ending for them. He surrendered to the authorities, was duly punished and returned to the services. He became an accountant and a respectable married man.

Meanwhile, the pattern of our wanderings during the next few months was now clear to us. We would load a cargo of what we vaguely called "high octane" oil in Abadan or Bahrein and take it to ports in Australia and elsewhere in the Far East, returning "light" ship to our storing port. We sailed down the Gulf, through the Straits of Hormuz, into the Arabian Sea and thence into the Indian Ocean, which I found at times of breath-taking beauty. The colours of its calm, limpid surface seemed to reflect the silken splendours of the countries whose shores it watered: India, Sri Lanka, Indonesia, Malaysia. I remember one evening in particular. The sunset sky had taken on a roseate brilliance, a sari embroidered on a backcloth of blue. Like an Indian dancer admiring herself in a mirror, every nuance of colour in the sky was reflected by the sea, until they merged into one seamless pattern and even the horizon was blurred.

So my love affair with the big breasted seas that had begun in the Atlantic continued as we sailed east. The sailors in an early Hollywood musical sang: "We saw the Atlantic and the Pacific, but the Atlantic wasn't romantic and the Pacific wasn't terrific", etc., but I found that each of the great oceans of the world had their own fascinating characteristics. The North Atlantic is justly famed for its stormy seas and even when the weather is clement the waves are still restless. The South Atlantic, on the other hand, is slower and calmer. Its billows are larger, slower, more expansive.

I never knew the Indian Ocean to be other than calm and serene, but I found the great Pacific huge and awesome, taking its restless nature from the bordering lands, the ancient civilisations of the Far East on one side, the aggressive modernity of the Americas on the other. Something of its size and global extent was, to me, characterised by the great albatrosses I watched gliding majestically over and through its massive billows.

At the other end of the scale the busy little Mediterranean takes its diversity from the varied lands that encompass it: the southern European countries from which Western civilisation sprang; the desert lands of north Africa; the religious turmoil of the Middle East. The sea can show itself very different in temper from the friendly environment so beloved by the modern holiday maker. One of the worst storms I ever experienced was when passing the isle of Malta, our poor little vessel being tossed about like an oil-can in a mill-race.

As on my first trip, however, I found a stark dichotomy between the natural beauty of our surroundings and the sometimes sordid tedium of life on board ship. Although we worked long hours there was still much time to kill during the journeys between ports that could last up to four weeks. We smoked endless cigarettes, of course, they being available sans any form of duty. Every cabin had an open box of Players, or round tins of the specially packed "ships Woodbines". We drank little alcohol, being limited to a few bottles of beer and one tot of rum when the bond opened once a week.

The old sea dogs devised a variety of hobbies to fill their time, using sea shells, fish bones, etc., some of them becoming quite skilled craftsman. It is known as scrimshaw and now sells well in auction sales. I remember watching a grizzled old bosun, with thick, weather-worn hands, producing fancy belts and other items from coloured cord on a wooden frame pierced with nails. I found my own way to pass the time writing verse and short stories, attempting to express how I felt about my environment, beautiful and otherwise.

I awoke one morning to find that my right knee had swollen to twice its normal size, crowned by an angry looking boil. When I tried to get out of my bunk the fluid sac hung on the knee-cap causing such excruciating pain that I fell on my back on the deck with my leg in the air. When help eventually arrived. I was put back on to my bunk, and remained there for several days more or less unattended. It appeared I had "housemaid's knee", which before then I had known only as a joke. This was no joke. Scrubbing hard decks without knee pads had produced its inevitable result. Crew members generally remained fit while at sea, which was just well as there was not only no doctor on board, but no hope of consulting one for days and even weeks. When the captain appeared on his weekly inspection I smiled apologetically for not being able to work. He looked at me in disgust and suggested that as I didn't appear to be cut out for sea life perhaps I should arrange to leave the ship at the next port.

The monotony of life on board was relieved on one notable occasion. The rust buckets in which we sailed were vulnerable to break-downs. Fortunately we carried a crew of engineers who were capable of dealing with most emergencies, such as the need to clean the vital piston rings when they clogged up and brought the ship's motor to a standstill. This happened once in the heart of the Indian Ocean and we hove-to so that it could be dealt with. The ship's second cook, who was also the baker, had run out of yeast, apparently because he had never been taught to grow an emergency supply on a potato. He tried baking bread without that essential ingredient and the result was predictable. The loaves were as heavy and solid as bricks, impervious to knife, saw or cleaver. As the ship wallowed in the calm blue sea, the crew amused themselves by dropping the loaves overboard to see how big a splash they would achieve.

This drew the attention of sharks, who circled around this invasion into their world to see if there was anything worth eating. Someone had the idea of fishing for them. Tackle was devised with a length of rope and a boat hook baited with a hunk of raw beef. It was lowered over the side and we watched as the rainbow pilot fish led the sharks to it. One magnificent monster turned its white belly upwards opened its great jaws and took the bait. Then it closed its mouth and went quiet while it digested what it had acquired.

With shouts of jubilation the men drew the creature out of the sea and over the rail. When it hit the deck, finding itself in a hard metal environment very different from the liquid world it had inhabited with such grace and freedom it flung its eight foot length about a space little more than 12 feet square and inhabited by up to a dozen men. In imminent danger from its snapping jaws they leapt in all directions, some hanging from stanchions, others hiding behind bollards. One took a metal bar and tried to stun it with blows to the head, which had little effect. Then someone to hit it on its tail, which strangely stilled it. A knife was brought and applied. The beautiful fish was still. The parasitic sucker fish that had been pulled up attached to its body writhed and splashed beside it.

Steaks were cooked from its flesh and soup from its fin, but they went into the officers' saloon and the crew saw none of them. The piston rings were cleaned, the ship renewed its laborious trek towards its destination and not even a ripple remained in the waters where the tiny drama had unfolded.

Our first port of call was Brisbane, Australia. We tied up alongside a berth in the mouth of a small river. For weeks we had been putting evaporated, or sweetened "condensed" milk into our coffee and tea. So my brother and I volunteered to go ashore and buy real milk freshly taken from the udders of a cow. We walked along a quay side and found a small café where a surprised young lady sold us a dozen pints.

We stayed only briefly to chat up the first pretty girl we had seen since we left England, but by the time we reached the ship we found to our dismay that it had cast off and was about to make its way up river to another destination. It was just moving away from the quay wall and many of the crew were lining the rail about eight feet above us, laughing at our predicament. We threw our bottles of milk up to them and they lowered ropes. We caught them and, swinging like apes, launching ourselves against the moving side of the ship, up over the rail and on to the deck. Looking back even now after all these years my heart sinks at what the consequences would have been if we had lost our grip and fallen between the quay and the moving ship.

Brisbane was a pretty little city and I remember a waterfront of pleasant suburban dwellings as we went up river. We were not able to stay long, however. Unlike traditional cargo ships it only takes a few hours to unload oil through the pipes into the tanks. The same was true when we visited other Australian ports, including Sydney and Perth. Only in Adelaide, South Australia, did we stay longer to deal with repairs to the engine. It was there that two members of the crew decided to "jump ship". A few hundred miles due north of the port in the heart of the Australian desert was Alice Springs, a booming mining town, where illegal immigrant workers were welcomed, with no questions asked.

Adelaide was also a pleasant city, with a substantial immigrant population, largely from the North of England, many of whom had been assisted by a British government subsidy. It was not very popular with the crews of visiting ships, however, as South Australia was known as a "wowser state", which meant its population was generally God-fearing and church going and did not tolerate the kind of facilities enjoyed by sailors in other parts of the world.

I, on the other hand, had a great time. I had recovered from my heart break and met Greta, a pretty girl with dark hair and a look reminiscent of a cinema favourite of the time, Gene Tierney. She introduced me to her family, first generation migrants from Sunderland in the north of England. Her father was very hospitable and one day took my brother and me to a horse race meeting. We boarded what started as a tram in the centre of town and, when it reached the outskirts, became a fast train along a fenced-off track, an admirable scheme for the suburbs of a small city.

As we approached the race track our host pointed out that the poor looking houses on the left of the railway were where "the honest jockeys lived", and the sumptuous dwellings on the other side of the track were the houses of the dishonest jockeys. He further demonstrated this state of affairs when we came to place our bets during a race, dissuading me from backing a favourite on the basis that it would undoubtedly be "pulled", which it certainly seemed to be!

My relationship with Greta could obviously never lead to anything. Mine was a transitory sailor's life and I was unlikely ever to return to Adelaide. She seemed to fall in love with me, however, and wrote to me for some time after I left. I would receive her tender letters when the ship docked at other ports. They were accompanied by photographs, sometimes rather superfluously of seascapes. Eventually, she realised the hopelessness of our situation and wrote a rather sad letter, bringing our gentle love affair to an end.

Many years later my brother told me he had suspicions that Greta's father had a concealed motive for being so hospitable to us. He had another daughter a few years older than Greta, who made approaches to him until she realised he had a fiancée back home. Suitable male partners were thin on the ground at that time in Australia, and the father presumably saw an opportunity to pass both his daughters off on to young sailors with marital potential

We visited ports in the Far East, calling first at Singapore, unloading at one of its many little islands. Then up to Shanghai in China, which was still a capitalist state ruled by Tchiang Kai Shek supported by the Americans. We anchored in the Yellow River, with its famous waterfront, the Bond. Ships of the US fleet were also there and we could hear their loud-hailers calling: "Now hear this, now hear this, all ashore who's going ashore", and "liberty guys to glamorise". My brother, who was to be married on his return to England, bought quantities of the finest silks at prices that hardly dented his sailor's salary.

We then travelled up to a port called Tsingtao, which contained a pocket of the US army surrounded by Communist forces. The troops were a merry band of young men, perhaps having a last fling before facing the enemy. We joined them in one of their canteens, drinking vodka and soda water out of small, almost identical bottles. One of their number was very drunk. He complained bitterly that what he was drinking was "rotten vodka". "Give me another bottle", he demanded. One of his companions warned me not to encourage him to drink any more. So I passed him a bottle of soda water. He drank from it and exclaimed: "Now that's better. That's good vodka".

We passed some of them in the street, on their way to a local brothel. They tried to persuade us to join them, but we refused. They were quite persistent and Eric had to explain that he was due to be married on his return to England and did not want to risk contracting venereal disease. "That's OK", they said, "You can always go to the prophylactic station". We preferred not to take the chance!

So we returned to the Gulf, which we were dreading. In May it had been blisteringly hot with the temperature constantly in the 100s. Our discomfort had been increased by the swarms of insects that invaded the ship. There were tiny midges that would sit on our arms and legs and gently move the hairs aside so that they could reach the skin and deliver a painful sting; and huge hornets that flew like tiny helicopters into our faces and terrified the life out of us. When we arrived in July, however, they had all gone. It appeared to be too hot for them, as I understand most species cannot endure a temperature much above 132°F. Our thermometers registered at least 135°F. We still had the company of the ubiquitous cockroaches, which inhabited spaces around our bunks and even under our pillows.

The heat was unendurable. The ship had been designed to serve the Shell facilities in the West Indies, unlike those of the rival company, BP, whose ships traded to the Gulf and had refinements that helped mitigate the excessive conditions. Their decks were wooden, whereas ours were metal. Theirs were covered with double awnings through which cool sea water could be hosed. They had more effective air-conditioning systems, whereas we only had "punkas" that were worse than useless as the air they blew out was hot.

Cabins were uninhabitable. If one was unwise enough to sit there within minutes a pool of sweat would appear in the lap. We took our bunk springs on to the upper deck, but there was little relief there. A hot wind blew sand from the desert, so we hung blankets up from stanchions as protection from it. We took salt tablets, but these tended to make some of us sick. The sweat came out on to our skins in the form of white powder.

We longed for the moment when we would set off for cooler climes, and there was even a rumour that we would be going home to England, but that proved to be false. Instead we had orders to make our way the relatively short distance to ports in the Red Sea: Malawi, Djibouti and Port Sudan. Although it was not as hot as the Gulf, it provided us with little relief unlike our trips further east and of course it meant we were back in the Gulf during August, the hottest month of the year.

It was as if this was the last straw. The crew was excused duties from eight in the morning till four in the afternoon, but some still had to work during the heat of the day. The catering department was expected to prepare and serve food and there were still matters that had to be attended to in the engine room One of the apprentice officers was the first to go down with heat stroke He was hastily put ashore into what we understood was an air-conditioned environment. Others followed until we had lost a third of our 32-man crew. I remember the third engineer coming up from a stint in the bowels of the ship, the sweat running through the black oil on his half-naked body. He threw a fit and squirmed on the deck, foaming at the mouth. They put him ashore with the others.

We were having a midday meal on the after deck when the third officer came and told us that the Chief Steward, Louis, had died. Some of the crew reacted with anger, believing it was a joke or a lie. But it was true. The gentle giant had succumbed. His body was placed in the refrigerator until we could bury him at sea.

Just as the ship sailed on this sad odyssey another of the catering staff fell ill. The only hope for him was that we would reach cooler weather in time to save him. He was put on a make-shift stretcher that night and carried round the ship trying to find some relief from the heat. I eventually fell asleep, still anxious for his fate, then woke to feel the cool breeze of the Arabian Sea on my face. We had passed through the Straits of Hormuz, Hell's Gate. I leapt up, pulled the blankets down hoping that now he would recover, which thankfully he did.

Chapter 10 – University of the sea

The voyage lasted a year and we returned to the UK with a few new faces on board, replacing those we had left ashore in Abadan recovering from heat stroke, or who had "jumped ship" in search of a better life in Australia. My brother was due to be married and, until he did, stayed at the family house. My elder brother, Fred, was still living there and his illness had reached a critical stage. He was not fully in control of himself and my parents felt threatened by him. They kept their bedroom door locked while they slept and one night he tried to break it down. Trembling they showed us a crack in the door. They seemed powerless to do anything about it. Eric and I agreed between ourselves that it could not be allowed to continue.

One day the whole family was sitting at table and my father made a joke that displeased Fred. He screamed at him and called him a common pig and other unpleasant names. Eric and I both stood up and confronted him. This made him aggressive. The situation was in danger of becoming violent. There was only one thing for it. We called the police and he was taken away to be incarcerated in Colney Hatch, a place that was then still called a lunatic asylum. Nowadays I believe the process is known as being sectioned. It might seem to have been a drastic way of proceeding, but in the event it was his saving. Once he realised he would not be able to return and dominate the family home he began to recover.

Eric had more than satisfied his national service requirement, but I still had a year of my conscription to serve. I had no desire to return to the Gulf but really had no alternative other than to apply for another position with the Shell Oil Company. I had no romantic entanglement to keep me ashore and was quite glad when I received an order to join another floating oil can. It was the MV Miranda, which was being reconditioned in Newcastle, on the River Tyne.

This was known as "working by", which meant two weeks in port, a rare treat for tanker crews. However, I had just spent a year in the hottest inhabited place on earth and this was January 1947, the coldest winter in the 20th century. My blood was thin and I found the cold almost unendurable. The snow was three feet deep. The ship was anchored in the middle of the river, which meant we had no protection from the biting wind. Whereas in the Gulf there had been no air-conditioning, on board this torture chamber there was no heating. I slept beneath eight layers of blankets and coats and still awoke in the mornings aching from the chill.

As usual on merchant ships, once my day's work was ended I could go ashore. Most of the crew would spend their evenings among the delights of Newcastle. One of my cabin mates, however, was a pleasant young man named Stuart, who had relatives in Gateshead on the south side of the river in County Durham. Regarded very much as the poorer relation of its prosperous neighbour, this nevertheless had the distinction of being the largest "town" in the country, an assessment presumably based on the size of the population.

When Stuart took me ashore to meet his family I could see how it gained its reputation. A little single-deck tram took us through seemingly endless ranks of terrace houses, typical of the urban dwellings that could be found in poorer areas throughout the country. They were described as slums, had outside toilets, no gardens and often large families crowded into insufficient accommodation. The people who lived in them, however, were the warmest, friendliest and most hospitable to be found anywhere in the globe. In common with their neighbours across the river, they were known as Geordies and had a unique accent that at times could become incomprehensible to a stranger.

Stuart had a vast extended family, with a Granny at its head and a wealth of aunts, uncles, cousins, nephews and nieces. Granny was a redoubtable little old lady, dressed in black, who kept the family in thrall and was treated with great respect by all. This was, of course, in the days before television and on a Saturday night the family would congregate in one side of a bar at the local pub, while a neighbouring family might fill another. They would drink a few glasses of beer, sing songs, sometimes in competition. That was as far as the competitiveness went, however. I do not recall any fights. No knives were wielded, no guns fired. A lot of beer was drunk, but it was hardly binge drinking and nobody seemed to find it necessary to bring the contents of their stomachs back up. When the pubs closed, as they all did then at 10.30, everyone would wend their way happily home. Granny did not like using public toilets and she was reputed to leave a little damp trail from the pub to her house!

To them I was something of a visiting celebrity, a presentable young man from the big city down south. On one occasion an aunt of Stuart's picked up the leather gloves I had been wearing and exclaimed: "Look at these!" She showed them proudly to the others. "Aren't they beautiful?" In fact they were quite ordinary, but after that to the whole family I was the young man with the beautiful gloves.

Rationing was still in force then and food in short supply, but our store rooms and refrigerators had already been stocked for our future journey so we had plenty. One night large steak pies were cooked for the officers and crew, but most of them went ashore to eat and they were being wasted. So we wrapped a couple up in brown paper and string and took them to the home of one of Stuart's aunts. We presented the parcel to her and told her it was a bird in a cage.

"What on earth do I want with a bird in a cage?" she exclaimed in her soft Geordie accent. "Haven't we got enough trouble feeding ourselves?"

Then we unwrapped it and their joy knew no bounds. Real steak in a real pie! They had eaten nothing like it for years.

There were several attractive young women among Stuart's cousins and shortly before we were due to sail he introduced me to one I had not met before. Her name was Doris. She was very pretty and slightly plump in what to me were all the right places. I berated Stuart for not introducing us before and even accused him of wanting to keep her for himself, which he found difficult to deny. Her mother had died a couple of years earlier and she lived with her father in what was rather grandly known as Low Fell House at the southern end of the Gateshead urban sprawl. He played the trumpet in the local theatre orchestra pit. She worked as a waitress in a small café.

We were immediately attracted to one another and spent a few happy hours together. I parted from her with great regret and wondered if this was going to be another case of frustrated love like Greta in Australia. I obviously could not predict that an all-demanding master fate would bring us together again in a scene that would be worthy of the closing shots in a Hollywood movie.

We sailed round the north coast of Scotland to avoid the storms that were still battering the Channel and southern England generally. We were bound for the West Indies and fortunately now there were no convoys, no U-boats to encounter, no sudden explosions as tankers disappeared from the sky-line. There was only the long sea-voyage ahead of us and the prospect of exciting forays among the fabled islands of the West Indies. The old-timers on board told tales of exciting nights ashore, where you drank rum and Coca-Cola to a calypso beat and went beachy-beachy with the ladies of Curacao.

I had served what was in effect my apprenticeship as cabin boy and acquired a "rating". I was now an Assistant Steward and my job was to look after the officers, keep their cabins clean and serve their meals. As on my previous ship the living and working superstructure was divided into two, with the officers' quarters and the bridge amidships and the crew accommodation aft with the engine and main storage rooms. The galley was also located at the furthermost rear of the ship so that food for the officers had to be carried from there along a catwalk over the well deck, constantly awash with waves from the wintry North Atlantic. I would have to wait for the water to subside and the ship to steady itself before risking the perilous trip, clutching food in open trays and billy cans held in a curious metal container.

I shared a cabin approximately eight feet by eight feet with my friend Stuart and a stout, rather older man from Southampton, whose name I have now forgotten. Two of the bunks were one above the other against the in-board bulk-head. I slept in the other located under the porthole. The only furniture in the room were three tall lockers and a chest of three drawers, which was also used as a table. It seems incredible now to think that we survived for weeks at sea in such conditions. There were, incidentally, several cats on board, one of which, a small black tom, adopted me and would sleep in the cabin.

Unlike my first trips on the North Atlantic, the weather was poor and for much of my spare time I found myself confined to my cabin. Having nothing else to do I took up the writing I had begun during the previous trip. One of the officers noticed this and told me about the Seafarers' Education Service. Apparently this ran correspondence courses through something called the College of the Sea. He arranged for a wireless message to be sent asking for information, which should reach the ship by the time we arrived at our first port.

Sure enough there was a package waiting for me in Curacao. It was from the director of the Service, Dr Ronald Hope, a man of great perception and sympathy to whom I have a debt of gratitude not only for my education at sea, but for his encouragement later when I went ashore. I replied saying I wanted to study English and was put in touch with a volunteer teacher named Phillip Gibbons. He was a lawyer on the staff of the National Coal Board, had read law at Oxford, but was also deeply interested in literature and drama. He wrote and asked me what I wanted to do, to which I replied that I wanted to read all the literature of all the countries in the world and all the periods of history. He replied that this was somewhat ambitious, but that he would at least try to take me through the main English tradition.

He sent me books of poetry and encouraged me to send him my efforts, which he commented upon, critically, but not unkindly. The Chief Steward allowed me to use a typewriter in his office and, thanks to having been taught touch-typing, I was able to beaver away at top speed. Unfortunately the noise disturbed the officers whose cabins were adjacent, and after complaints the privilege was withdrawn and I had to revert to hand writing.

Looking back I realise what an immensely important factor this experience was in my life. It was probably the equivalent of a year at a university. Although I worked 12 hours a day there was still much time to kill and without the distractions I might have encountered on a university campus I was probably able to concentrate more on actual studying than many a student. In addition I had the encouragement of a personal tutor who, although geographically separated, obviously had my education and potential development at heart.

Curacao was then a far cry from the tourist paradise it has since become. Oil was refined there and on other nearby islands, such as Trinidad, having been carried from the wells of Venezuela in mini-tankers. My principal memory of it were the dockside bars that were obviously there to cater for sailors who had spent several weeks at sea and were thirsty for stimulation of various kinds.

When ships were at sea liquor was severely rationed to the crew. Once a week the "bond" was opened by the Chief Steward and we were sold a quantity of cigarettes or tobacco, a few bottles of beer and a tot of rum, which we had to drink there to ensure we did not store it to consume at some potential binge later. So being released from the thraldom of the ship to go ashore the crew tended to overdo the imbibing, something I fear I was guilty of on my first night ashore.

A popular song of the moment extolled the virtues of "rum and Coca Cola", sung I believe by the Andrew Sisters and presumably sponsored by the manufacturer of the drink. The bar we visited, however, did not mix them in some kind of cocktail. Instead they sold us small flat bottles of local rum, accompanied by bottles of coke, and left us to mix them according to taste. As a teenager I had enjoyed the occasional tipple and been known to become mildly intoxicated, but I was ill prepared for the impact of neat West Indian rum on my immature stomach. I was carried back to the ship, up the companionway and on to the deck, where I was left to stand on my own feet. Unfortunately, the gravity of my situation made itself felt and I measured my length in a pool of oil. In preparation for shore leave in place of the stewards' jacket, sweaty tee-shirt and smelly trousers I had donned a white shirt, smart pale blue trousers and multi-hued shoes. All were soaked in the horrible black stuff, as were my face, hands and hair. The next morning I responded to the laughter of the crew by claiming I had only drunk one bottle of rum and it must have been laced with something. They pointed out I had drunk not one, but three bottles of the fiery stuff and hardly any Coca Cola.

The following night my low-life cultural baptism was to continue. The men were going ashore again to enjoy what they called "beachy-beachy". I wasn't entirely sure what this comprised, except that it involved women and sex, but I was anxious to demonstrate that I was man enough to join them. I was, anyway, curious to discover what it was all about.

We went to the same bar, where a gaggle of laughing women had gathered. They quickly disposed themselves among chosen members of the crew. They were of varying ages and I was perturbed to find that I had the attention of a dark, swarthy lady who was somewhat older than I. and whose interest in me was certainly not maternal.

A number of taxis arrived and we were all driven off to the seashore where we dispersed among strategically placed breakwaters. The only light came from the moon and its reflection in the sea. My companion took me to a spot on the sand among the rocks, lay back and lifted her black voluminous dress. Then she spread her legs to expose the delights she undoubtedly thought I desired. Like Adonis I "looked and saw more wounds than one". Adonis fled, taking advantage of his god-like status. I was a mere merchant seaman with nowhere to flee and was rooted to the spot.

She laughed and beckoned me to her with waves of her plump hands. My experience of the female sex had been with girls like Iris in Enfield, Greta in Adelaide and Doris in Gateshead, with none of whom had I experienced the full joys of sex. If I was to lose my virginity I wanted it to be in a romantic encounter with someone like them, not confronted by that monstrous cavern. The matronly lady on the rocks started muttering something about her money. I hastily drew out my wallet and thrust a couple of notes towards her. She took them then seized my arm with her other hand, pulling me towards her perhaps determined not to lose the opportunity of sex with a handsome young sailor. She was quite strong and I feared that, at the least, I would find myself grappling with this fearsome creature. Fortunately my honour was saved by what I might in my later literary life regard as a d*eus ex machina.*

Whether at some prearranged signal between the women and the drivers or because the local constabulary had made an appearance, the taxis suddenly put on all their headlights and blew their horns. All over the beach women could be seen leaping up, laughing and chattering, pulling up their drawers, lowering their skirts and dragging the men who were hastily buttoning trousers and tucking in shirts. They ran towards the lights. I offered my hand to my disappointed paramour, but she stood up, pushed me aside and preceded me to the waiting vehicle.

The next day I once again had to face the derision of

some crew members, who seemed to be aware that I had not taken full advantage of the facilities offered on the beach. I feared they were beginning to regard me as homosexual, and was concerned at the possibility of that in the long weeks on this crowded ship. Fortunately there was soon to be an encounter in another port from which I would regain their respect.

We set sail bound for South America and I soon found myself gazing at the coastline of Brazil, a fabled country that had featured in so many famous Hollywood films. One of the latest was the Walt Disney animation *The Three Caballeros* that had been released in the UK shortly before I left. The principal characters were Donald Duck and a parrot called Joe Carioca, who was trying to persuade Donald to visit the exotic lands of South America.

"Ah! Pato Donald", he would say, "have you ever been to Bahia? What! You've never been to Bahia! Then you must go to Bahia."

As we made our slow way down the coast I tired the crew by interminably repeating this phrase. Then the ship's engine suffered one of its frequent break-downs. It could not be repaired at sea and there was nothing for it but to put into port. And what port would that be? Bahia! Members of the crew forgave me for irritating them with my constant repetition, believing me responsible for some kind of miracle. Moreover, we were going to be allowed ashore, to a fabled town that had been the location for a famous film. We could not have been more excited if we were going to visit Hollywood itself.

We went ashore first during the afternoon break in order to reconnoitre. It turned out to be a delightful town in the Spanish colonial style. It was very quiet in what would have been siesta time. There were four of us in our group and as we walked around a pleasant, sunlit square we stopped at the spectacle of an angel who was gliding towards us with the grace of a ballet dancer. As she came up to us we raised our hats and she returned the courtesy with a smile that rivalled the sun in its brilliance.

"Hullo boys", she said with just a hint of an accent. "Are you from the tanker just in town".

We nodded, probably looking stupid. Her smile broadened.

"And are you looking for somewhere to go, perhaps tonight?"

Again we nodded, still without demonstrating any intelligence.

"Then you must come to the Fiesta night club. You will be very welcome."

And she handed out a leaflet, which I took as if it were holy writ.

"*Muchas gracias*", I said. She looked at me in astonishment, then laughed and made her way down the street, watched by our adoring eyes.

We returned to the ship, served the evening meal and dressed with the care and pleasure that weeks of dirt and privation give to such simple preparations. Bahia was not a regular shipping port and there were no facilities serving the needs of sailors. So a number of us decided to take advantage of whatever the Fiesta had to offer. One of our officers, who had visited the port before warned us that it was a smart venue and we were to behave ourselves with diplomatic politeness.

It did indeed turn out to be very elegant, with a real South American band playing real South American music and couples dancing demurely on the tiny dance floor. We had been issued with only a small allocation of pesos, enough for no more than a bottle of beer apiece, but we sat and drank our beer, listened to the music and watched the elegant dancers.

A favourite piece of music in those days was the song *Brazil* and I thought what a wonderful experience it would be if we could persuade a real Brazilian band to play it for us. I beckoned the waiter over. Although I had paid little attention to the study of Spanish at school I thought I knew enough to make the waiter understand that I liked the song

Brazil and wanted to hear it: *"Comprende? Quiero Brazil mucho. Para mi, prego?"* He did not seem to understand a word. Then one of my companions asked me what language I was trying to speak. I told him Spanish and he pointed out that Brazil was the only Latin American country that spoke Portuguese.

I did not think there could be all that difference so I persisted with the waiter until he scratched his head and went away to return with somebody who may have been a head waiter. I repeated my request with similar lack of understanding. He was replaced by a very grand gentleman in an evening suit who seemed to get quite angry. He disappeared and I was derided by the other crew members until one of them drew our attention to someone who had entered the room, was talking to the manager and looking in our direction. It was the woman who had spoken to us in town earlier.

We gazed at her as she crossed the room. She was coming towards our table. She was coming to me. She stopped by my side and. I got unsteadily to my feet.

"Senor", the vision intoned, "You want Brazil?"

"Yes, yes", I stuttered, "Brazil, *si usted gusta.*"

The goddess drew herself up, seeming to become taller, even more statuesque.

"I", she announced "am Brazil".

She smiled, raised an imperious arm and beckoned.

"Come with me", she said.

I went in stunned silence, while the rest of the crew cheered and clapped. She took me to what was obviously her dressing room, sat and adjusted her make-up in the mirror and invited me to sit by her. Then she asked about myself, where I was from, did I have a girlfriend. She was very charming and I felt sure I could easily fall in love with her. She asked how I knew her name and I explained it was the song I wanted to hear. She laughed, got up and kissed me on the cheek. Then she went to the door, opened it and gestured me to leave.

"Enjoy your evening", was all she said. I did not know

whether to be disappointed or elated. My shipmates, however, were in no doubt. They greeted me like a returning hero. Then the band struck up some commanding chords. Its leader made an announcement that was met with applause from the audience. On to the little stage came our beautiful lady greeted by more applause. She said something in Portuguese, followed by translation: "for our amigos from across the water". Then she sang "Brazil". It could not have been better if Bing Crosby, Fred Astaire and Rita Hayworth had been up there on the rostrum. Despite our relatively impoverished state the management treated us with great courtesy. Perhaps they were already anticipating that their little town would one day become one of the top tourist destinations in the world.

I did not dance at the Fiesta. It was not that kind of club, but our next port of call was Montevideo and I made a point of returning to the night club where I had danced with Musetta. As we went through the door there was a little scream of delight from the dance floor. She left her partner, rushed up to me, threw her arms around my neck and kissed me. She had remembered me after all that time. We danced together again and when she asked me if I had *dinero* I felt able to say yes. She took me behind a partition, where she sat me down and performed what would nowadays be known as a lap-dance. She seemed to enjoy it as much as I did!

Sadly, in Montevideo, my cabin mate and good friend Stuart woke one morning with a lump and severe pain in his groin. He was taken ashore to hospital, where a hernia was diagnosed. He would need an immediate operation and we would have to sail without him. His replacement was a sharp-faced, red-headed Scotsman named Runciman. He joined us with something of a reputation as a roughneck and it was said he had used a knife on a fellow seaman. He was a poor substitute for Stuart and made no attempt to ingratiate himself with his new companions. He and I, in particular, did not get on well together

I felt he was constantly challenging me to react to his behaviour and one day he succeeded. I invited him on to the after deck where he thought he would have an easy contest. He was wrong. As I have intimated before my looks belied my pugilistic abilities. When his face became bruised and bloodied he dropped his fists in a gesture of defeat.

I could have inflicted further pain, but that is not in my nature. Instead, I led him to a wash room and helped bathe his wounds. Later one of the senior officers asked how he had been injured. I told him he had been hit by a door. "What on both eyes?" he queried. Anyway Runciman must have felt that his pride had been damaged as well as his face and at the next port of call he jumped ship, never to be seen by me again.

His departure meant that I now had the luxury of sharing the cabin with only one other man. He was a pleasant enough fellow, married and intending to spend his working life as a seaman. I wondered what sort of wedded bless there could be for a couple, one half of which spent up to a year at a time away from home. The danger this presented to marital bliss was demonstrated when the ship put in at another of the West Indian islands, Aruba.

We were visited at night by the local ladies whose business it was to attend to the needs of itinerant voyagers. One of them came to our cabin and displayed her wares to me. As before I did not find this particularly vivifying so she turned to my cabin mate. At first he insisted that he had someone waiting for him at home. When she lowered her price he began to find her more attractive.

She climbed perilously on to his bunk. I put the light out, went to bed and tried to ignore the grunts and gasps. Then I heard another noise. It was my cat scratching and mewing at the cabin door. I got up in the dark and opened it enough to let the animal in. Then I went back to bed and tried to sleep, but again it was to prove impossible. Suddenly, there was a scream from the woman, a cry from my shipmate: "That bloody cat". These were followed by a brief scuffle, and the sound of someone falling on the deck. I got up, switched on the light to find him standing over the prostrate form of the lady.

"What the hell did you want to let thing in for?" he demanded. He helped her to her feet and ensured that any damage to her person or her dignity was assuaged with an appropriate remuneration. She left and we both went back to bed. He was obviously furious with me and kept on about it in the dark until I suggested:

"This was probably divine intervention. Or perhaps in this case feline intervention"

"What the hell are you talking about?"

"Well,. Look at it this way. It might have saved your marriage. How would your wife like it if you went home with a dose of the claps, or even worse?"

He did not reply and I never found out if the marriage survived or not.

The voyage lasted a year and once again we docked in the Tyne. I thought I would go ashore and see if there was any news of Stuart. I caught the tram in Gateshead and got off near to the place where most of his family lived. It was about halfway up the hill towards Doris's home in Low Fell. As I walked along the dimly lit street a female figure was coming towards me. We stopped and faced one another for a moment. Then she said: "Is that Leslie?" I asked: "Is that Doris?" She came up to me and we embraced. Through the passing of time and over thousands of miles of ocean we had been drawn to one another by who knows what accident of fate. Sadly, the same force, whatever it is, eventually caused us to part, but that does not detract from the romance of that moment.

Chapter 11 - Ye olde order changeth

It was 1948. I had completed my three year national service commitment to the Merchant Navy and could remain home. Rationing was still in force, not only for food, but for other necessities, such as clothes, but London was shaking its great head from the battering it had received and the arguments were beginning about what to build and where.

Winston Churchill had led the nation out of the jaws of defeat into what at one time seemed an impossible victory over the massed Nazi and Fascist forces. It might have been expected that he would continue to do so in the subsequent peace, but as this was democratic Britain he had called a general election – no doubt with the full expectation that he would win. As history shows he miscalculated. A Labour Government came into office with a large majority and a manifesto to change the shape of British society forever. Many British citizens – my father among them – were devastated.

The National Health Service was established and the comprehensive national welfare scheme proposed in the Beveridge report accepted. Various service industries were nationalised. India and other former colonies were granted their independence, so ushering in a Commonwealth of Nations. Under the Marshall Plan the USA contributed greatly towards the regeneration of Europe. Britain joined NATO and the Council of Europe, which eventually led to the establishment of the European Union

My old friends were slowly returning from the various branches of national service in which they had served and, like me, were trying to pick up the fabric of their lives again. Two of them had joined the Merchant Navy as apprentices and had not had time even to achieve officer status. One had been in the Royal Air Force, another in the army. Facilities for young people that may have been neglected during the war were revived, so there was ice-skating, swimming, dancing and, of course, many cinemas. None of us had cars, but transport was no problem. Most of us cycled. The Underground was an unfailing source of cheap, easy transport, as were buses and trolley buses.

My mother and father were now living alone in the old house on which they had been able to buy a long lease for a very modest sum. Later they acquired the freehold for a further trifling figure. The cost of the whole process probably did not run into four figures. That house is now reputed to be worth over a million pounds. My brother Eric was married and living in the neighbouring borough of Tottenham, where he owned a small corner grocery shop. Fred was still in hospital being treated for his mental condition. He once told me how painful and distressing some of this treatment was, involving as it did electric shocks directly into the brain. My sister Edna had found that her husband's extensive absences from the marital home were not entirely accounted for by the needs of his work. She still lived in the Surrey cottage while her divorce was being negotiated.

Not yet being in employment it was important for me to live frugally. One way to achieve this was to give up smoking. Cigarettes had been essential in passing the tedious weeks at sea, but there they were available at practically give-away prices. Ashore they were beginning their upward spiral and already cost 2s 10d for a packet of 20. Also they were in short supply. Customers had to queue for them and tobacconists hid them under their counters. One day I developed toothache. I do not believe I had ever visited a dentist before, but I obviously had to do so now. He removed a tooth and instructed me not to smoke for three days. I was half-way through a packet of 20 and decided that if I could give cigarettes up for three days I could give them up for good. So I did. It was one of the best decisions I ever made. It is presumably one of the reasons why I am able to edit this as I approach 90, still sing in choirs and until quite recently managed 18 holes on the golf course. My father, on the other hand, succumbed to lung disease before he was 60, leaving his non-smoking wife to outlive him by 30 years.

I needed to find work, but the problem was what sort of work should it be. After three years travelling the world in the open air I found it difficult to envisage a return to an office. I thought of going to sea on a whaler, or one of the grain ships that still travelled under sail to the Far East. I decided, however that I had had enough of the hardships such a life would offer. I would like open-air work and considered working on the land, but I was not cut out to be a farmer. Then I remembered the advice given me by the father of a former girl-friend. He was manager of a large insurance company's local branch office and had urged me to consider taking it up as a career, perhaps seeing me as a potential bread-winner for his daughter. He described how he started work as a representative, travelling and visiting potential and actual clients. It was reasonably outdoor.

I went to his office and asked his advice, half expecting that he might offer me a job. I was disappointed. He told me I would have to begin by gaining experience in the head office of a large insurance company. He recommended Pearl Assurance. It was not what I was looking for, but it was work. I applied, was accepted and turned up one Monday morning to start at its extensive offices in Holborn.

This proved to be something of a culture shock. The large room I worked in was furnished by a series of long desks at each of which six book-keepers worked, sitting on high stools. We were the indoor equivalents of outdoor representatives selling and managing what was known as "industrial insurance". They would call on domestic premises to be paid the small amounts of the customers' premiums, which would be recorded on forms submitted to Head Office. Each desk in the room represented a region. Each operator was responsible for a group of representatives.

There was a weekly routine. When the forms were received on Tuesdays the payments were recorded by date-stamping the insured names in vast ledgers. Each form was checked and turned over to make way for the next and the entry in the ledger was stamped. This process lasted for more than two days. Although the manual operation was largely mechanical, if a mistake was made it could have serious consequences as it would indicate that someone had paid when they had not, or vice versa. So, like some great percussive tattoo, for hours on end the thumping of 200 rubber stamps on ink pad and ledger would be the only sound that was heard in that vast room – turn, thump, thump, turn, thump, thump.

After two weeks I had had enough. I approached the supervisor who sat in isolated state behind a glass partition and said I wanted a different job. I would like, I said, to be a representative outside, perhaps selling insurance. The mighty potentate threw up his hands in ridicule. That was something that could only be achieved after a great deal of experience, much of it gained by doing my present job.

"Go back to your work, young man", he said. "If you apply yourself and keep your nose clean after a few years you might be considered for such a position, always providing of course that one became vacant". I went back to my seat among the ranks of turn/thumpers with a feeling of despair. Was this to be my future for the next "few years"? Scrubbing decks might have been menial and lead to housemaids' knee, but at least there was the prospect of a few days in a glamourous foreign port. Even the Abadan run seemed preferable.

Then just as it seemed my life was to be mired in tediousness and boredom I received a telephone call from my mentor at the College of the Sea, Philip Gibbons. He had been approached by a young university graduate who had set up a publishing house in the West End of London. He was looking for a general assistant to undertake a variety of jobs, including book-keeping, invoicing and – what was more attractive to me - occasional editorial work. Was I interested? Was I! The money offered represented a small drop in salary – I think from £3 to

£2.10s a week - but that was of no consequence. I attended an interview and was offered the job immediately. I visited my supervisor again and gave him my fortnight's notice. He looked at me in astonishment.

"You can't do that!" he cried. "Nobody, but nobody, has ever left employment at this Company after only six weeks."

When word went round that I was leaving I received surreptitious visits from my erstwhile colleagues who congratulated me. One of them was my immediate line boss, who sidled up to me furtively, looking over his shoulder as if fearing he would be overheard by big brother. Whispering in my ear, he told me he had been with the company since the early 1930s. He had returned after his conscription in the army only to find that promotion had been offered to younger men. Since then he had progressed no further than presiding over the work of six underlings. He lived now, he said, only for his retirement in a few years' time. From then on I decided I would never allow my life to be conscribed by any organisation.

It was the beginning of a new life. My employers turned out to be two very enterprising young men publishing books in the classical and general categories under the name of the senior partner Nicholas Kaye. The classics comprised reprints of Jane Austen in attractive black hard-back covers with end-papers of fashion prints from the period. Among the general titles were Ben Hogan on golf and the first book to be published with recipes for pressure cooking, just introduced to the nation's kitchens.

They also published the Manchester Cookery Book, from which it appeared a recipe had been drawn for the christening cake of the baby Prince of Wales. As the book was already on booksellers' shelves, it was necessary to design a "wrap-around" with an appropriate advertising slogan to be used on all copies. The staff was asked for suggestions. I proposed "Fit for a Prince", which to my delight was accepted. So far as I am aware the slogan had never been used before, but it has been very popular since, so I think I am justified in claiming the copyright!

The company was located in Kaye's home at No.1 Trebeck Street a very fashionable Mayfair address, so he could not have been short of a penny or two. The offices were on the ground floor with domestic premises above. The family, I recall, had two black giant poodles, who moved freely about the building as if they owned it and were walked by the family maid. I worked in the basement, which also served as a storeroom for some of the stock. I did the book-keeping, wrapped and posted parcels of books, provided occasional copy for advertisements, and read proofs. I was even allowed to work as sub-editor on the Athlete, which we published on behalf of the Amateur Athletic Association. No doubt the company got its money's worth from me, but I did not care. In my dark little basement I was in heaven!

Meanwhile, my thirst for literary knowledge increased. It was as if I was trying to make up for all the wasted years. I read avidly works of all periods and from many countries, Greece, Rome, Italy, France, Germany, Spain although sadly always in translation. It was the time when Penguin was publishing its wonderful series edited by E. P. Rieu. There were also the series of classics in hard back published by Everyman, not to mention a reasonably well-stocked local public library. Nothing was too daunting:: War and Peace, Anna Karenina, Don Quixote, the Decameron, Arabian Nights, the short stories of Tchekov, de Maupassant, Somerset Maugham, Thurber, et al. Then there were the tragedies of Sophocles, Aeschylus, Euripides and the comedies of Aristophanes, leading me to Homer and the Greek philosophers. I read both books of the Bible and worked my way through the whole of Shakespeare

On a more personal side I had kept up my relationship by correspondence with Doris, and eventually it was agreed that she should join me in London. Looking back I realise it was a brave move for her. She had grown up in a close provincial community, with an extended family group, keeping house for her elderly father. Coming down to the big city was a major step and one that I have always appreciated. It was sad that after such a promisingly romantic onset our relationship was not to last, but perhaps that was inevitable from the turmoil that my life was to become in later years. We got engaged and very much wanted to marry, but preferred not to do so until we had a place of our own. Accommodation was in short supply, however, and it seemed a hopeless situation.

One day we learnt that the upstairs flat of a small terrace house in Brixton, South London, was available for rent. We hastened over the river and met the landlord and landlady, who lived on the ground floor. At first they refused to accept us because we were not married, but we quickly said we were engaged to be married within days. They accepted us and we hastily made arrangements for the wedding. In those days Brixton was a typical London inner suburb, where accommodation was cheap. It is unlikely that a young couple in a situation like ours would be able to afford it today.

We spent a pleasant time there until, after about 18 months, my father began to suffer from the inevitable smoking-related illness. He was taken to hospital, where Doris and I visited him. On one occasion he struggled for breath and seemed to find our presence irksome. After a while he whispered to me: "Take her away". I did so and that was the last time I saw him alive. My mother was now alone in the large house so we went to live there with her.

After a happy couple of years with Nicholas Kaye I left to become a sub-editor on the weekly Nursing Times, published by Macmillan's on behalf of the Royal College of Nursing. The editor, assistant editor and a journalist were all nurses. They were responsible for writing and commissioning the material to be published in the magazine. I worked with two other professional sub-editors, one of them part-time. Our task was to edit the copy before it went down to the press, check the galley proofs, produce the "paste-ups" that indicated the lay-out for the printer, and pass the final page proofs.

We often found it necessary to challenge the grammatical and stylistic efforts of both the senior editorial staff and the learned medical practitioners who comprised the magazine's contributors. This created a certain degree of tension, particularly when it was felt we had altered the medical significance of a passage in order to present it in what we thought was a reasonably grammatical and lucid form.

One of the attractions for me was that the magazine included an "off-duty page" and we received press tickets so that we could publish reviews of West End theatre productions and concerts, as well as art exhibitions. I took advantage of these whenever I could and if I did not have a free ticket for something I paid for it. Prices were then within the reach of all. The director of the Seafarers' Education Service made use of my enthusiasm for critical writing by asking me to contribute regular theatre reviews for "The Seafarer" a magazine he published every quarter. He was very kind about my abilities in this field, describing me as a rival to Ivor Brown, who was the doyen of theatre reviewers in those days! My criterion of excellence was George Bernard Shaw, whose "Our Theatre in the Nineties" I devoured. He is sadly neglected these days, but I regard him as one of our greatest prose writers and believe his influence as a playwright was profound.

My interest in the theatre took a more practical form when I became involved in amateur dramatics. I had maintained contact with my tutor from the College of the Sea, Philip Gibbons, and we became quite good friends, although we could not have been more different in background and personality. A kindly, gentle man of uncertain age, he was the only genuinely asexual man I have ever known. Unmarried, he had no intimate relationship with either gender. His closest friend was another bachelor, who shared many of his aesthetic interests, but was overtly homosexual, so that they made an interesting, but somewhat unusual couple.

I was grateful to Philip for his tutorship at sea and later introduction to the publishing world and enjoyed meeting him at his Adam-designed flat in central London. He told me of his time at Oxford University, where, although he read law he developed a deep interest in the theatre and became involved with the renowned Oxford University Dramatic Society (OUDS). His legal training had led him into what was obviously a well-paid job in the Civil Service. To satisfy his interest in drama he had established an amateur dramatic society in – of all places - the East End of London. Learning of my interest in the theatre he asked me if I would like to join as an actor and possible director.

Under Philip's direction the group had a strong educational element, confining its choice of plays to the classics or those with literary merit, rather than the programme of popular murder mysteries and comedies favoured by many amateurs. His very reasonable argument was that, whatever the quality of the acting and production, at least the audience benefited from a work of some literary and historical merit. The group met in a Society of Friends hall off Brick Lane in a side street called Barnet Grove, rehearsing once a week and performing for local people two or three times a year.

So I joined the group and quickly found I was satisfying a desire that had obviously been latent in me since childhood. When I stepped out in front of an audience, clothed in the personality of a stage character I felt in command. Our programme was inspirational. We produced the Antigone of Sophocles; Shaw's Pygmalion and Arms and the Man; Tchekov's Three Sisters; our own translation of Moliere's Tartuffe and the plays of the Spanish Quintero brothers. I acted in some productions and directed others. Sometimes I did both at once. As a director I found I could mentally envisage the setting and the actors' places in it. My new wife joined me, making, I remember, a particular impact as a beautiful Elmire in Tartuffe.

Some of the pieces attempted were obviously technically challenging for a group with such meagre resources. Bernard Shaw, in particular, wrote Pygmalion when regiments of backstage workers were on hand to change a setting from Covent Garden to an Edwardian interior in a matter of seconds. It took us 20 minutes and was not helped by the failure of a particularly important light source! The Three Sisters is designed for a dinner scene to take place on an inner stage, which was impossible with our handkerchief of a playing area. Producing Antigone proved easier. We moved the acting area into a different hall with no stage and a full sized snooker table, which we disguised as an altar. When my wife made her entrance dressed in the traditional chiton, it was to the accompaniment of comments from the audience that she seemed to be wearing her nightdress!

They were, however, lovely friendly audiences. In those days the area was populated by traditional Londoners living in rows of terrace houses similar to those in Doris's home town of Gateshead. The residents were quite house-proud and could be seen scrubbing their front door-steps or polishing the brass door furniture. Condemned as slums, however, they were later demolished to make way for what were regarded as more desirable high-rise dwellings destined to have such a disastrous impact on community life. They were not always sure what to make of our offerings, but there was no doubt performers and audience alike had a great deal of fun out of them.

I did not realise it as the time, but my involvement in the group was creating a conflict of interest in me that would never be resolved. On the one hand I was anxious to develop and use the writing skills that had been apparent since childhood. On the other there was the gravitational pull of the theatre. I did not see how this could be more than an impossible dream. People who worked on the professional stage went to drama schools like RADA, or LAMDA, or were members of hieratical families. Employment opportunities were limited and uncertain and I needed to earn a living.

This last was a major consideration for me as I was about to become a father. Like many young potential mothers my wife viewed the prospect of giving birth with trepidation, particularly as she had been brought up in a close social environment where childbirth was still accompanied by a certain amount of superstition and fear. Moreover, she had no mother or close family to support her.

One of the benefits of being a journalist, however, is that one often has the advantage of gaining an insight into areas of activity confined to the expert. When she became pregnant I was still working on the Nursing Times, which published a series of articles on what was called "birth without fear", designed specifically to remove some of the ill-informed ideas surrounding what it suggested was a natural function. It was based largely on the writings of Grantly Dick-Read, who was currently practising the principles he promoted at University College Hospital. Admission to the unit was limited, but first-time mothers were generally welcomed. I don't know whether my position on the magazine influenced the result, but Doris was accepted as a patient and the programme of relaxation exercises was a great help to her. In the event, the birth proved a happy experience for both of us and our son Graham was born.

Chapter 12 – Magazines and plays

The work of editing a magazine in those days would no doubt seem very strange to those involved in publishing today. Even as I "type" these words I am aware how much the computer has taken over the skills we exercised with such diligence. I was still a typographical novice when I became a sub-editor of the Nursing Times and I had a great deal to learn. I was fortunate to find myself working alongside an experienced sub-editor, Phil Sidey, who was not only prepared to help initiate me into the mysteries of the work, but was also a pleasant associate. I enrolled in a course for aspiring editors run by the London School of Printing, no doubt to ensure we were prepared for the time when we worked with skilled printers.

We were shown the trays, or galleys, that had been used to hold type metal since printing began, and the hand "sticks" used before the advent of mechanical composing machines. We were introduced to the Linotype system, which produced lines of type in metal slugs in a single operation and was then the principle equipment used to print newspapers and magazines. There was also the older Mono-type process, which produced individual characters on two separate machines and was regarded as more suitable for better quality book production.

We learnt the different type faces and the appropriate ways of applying them, according to the subject matter and the type of paper being used. There were differences between centuries old faces like Garamond, still in use, but perhaps more suitable for traditional, formal work; and modern ones like Bodoni with hair-line serifs, which should not be used on paper with a glossy or matted surface because in both instances the serifs could be obscured. We were introduced to the work of Eric Gill, one of this country's greatest sculptors, who revolutionised type design with a face having no serif, still known to most computer users today.

Most importantly we were taught the importance of reading and manipulating the galley proofs. They had to be read with care and marked-up with a range of symbols to indicate corrections. Then they were cut up and pasted on to pages, with headlines, sub-lines and spaces for the pictures, black-and-white photographs, which we edited on the reverse so that they could be made into "half-tone" blocks of the correct size to fit the editor's page design. From these paste-ups page proofs were produced to be compared with the galleys and finally "passed for press".

Having completed the course I felt I was qualified to seek advancement in the magazine world and applied for the position of Assistant Editor to an export trade magazine with the unusual title of Mercantile Guardian. I say unusual because like most people I identified the word Mercantile with ships, but in this case it had the older meaning of "merchanting", or trade.

Glancing at a copy while I was waiting for my interview with the editor, I thought its appearance also belonged to a bygone age and I wondered what I might be letting myself in for. Ron Rowney, the editor, however, turned out to be totally aligned with modern times. He asked me if I drank and, thinking he wanted me to demonstrate my abstemiousness, I assured him I did so only in moderation. He took this for a "no" and said: "Pity, that's the best thing about this job".

When I showed him a sample of my work in the Nursing Times containing an article with particularly lurid pictures of a medical procedure he went somewhat pale and swore softly. I think he thought it important to offer me a way of escape from such a gruesome environment so he took me on and I found myself introduced to the world of economics.

Once again the magazine would be regarded with astonishment by those involved in the present- day media world. Printed entirely in black on white it had a dull air-force blue cover that never varied except for the date. When the galley proofs came up from the printers they were cut either into articles or into small news items that were attached to strips of paper, then pasted on to measured pages like wall-paper. The magazine contained no pictures. Each issue ran to approximately 350 pages, of which the advertisements filled more than 300, covering the vast range of products British manufacturers were selling throughout the world

The editorial content fell into two main categories: what may be described as the learned articles on economics and trade; and short news items and lists of interest to the trader. The editor wrote most of the articles, with regular contributions by a free-lance journalist. I was responsible for the rest, producing scores of short paragraphs, giving details of products for sale, visiting trade buyers, changes of address, etc.

Very occasionally I was allowed to test my journalistic skills with a "short feature" occupying about a quarter of a page. Rowney never allowed me to write anything that might be interpreted as an expression of opinion. He obviously regarded himself as an expert in economics, although we seldom discussed them and I was never sure what his political leanings were. Looking back I suspect he was a pre-Thatcherite, regarding the profit motive as the principal and most satisfactory system for saving mankind.

Yet in spite of its unlikely title and format there is no doubt the magazine, published monthly, played an important part in the economic environment of the day. This was when the people of Britain were being urged to "export or die" and the MG was something of an official journal to the export trade. Its success and even fame in that area of business also owed a great deal to the accompanying Mercantile Year Book and Directory of Exporters, which was regarded as the exporter's bible, containing as it did the names and contact details of export merchants and their international clients

The publishing house itself was something of a phenomenon. With just those two publications, it successfully provided a livelihood for two brothers who comprised the chairman and managing director; the son of one of them, also a director; an advertising department with a manager and staff; a distribution team of a manager and several assistants; the editor of the Year Book and his secretary; the advertisement manager of the Year Book and his secretary; and the editorial staff of the magazine, which comprised the editor, myself and his secretary. A company secretary attended the office a couple of days a week.

Rowney's system of writing was unusual to say the least and quite in keeping with the character of the man. He never arrived in the office before 10.15 am, having commuted from his home on the coast in Eastbourne, via Waterloo, to our offices in Bishopsgate. Before he arrived his secretary would have selected from the Financial Times, The Economist magazine and other similar learned journals information on trade and economics, which she thought would be of interest and importance to him and might form the basis of articles. She would cut these out and display them on his desk for him to study.

He would dictate an article or two to her, check any she had previously prepared and at approximately 12.30 would put any proofs for reading in his brief case and disappear to Fleet Street. There he would meet for consultation with our regular freelance contributor, Johnny Wood, together with other journalists in a Fleet Street pub. His day would finish at 3.0 pm, when he left for Waterloo to catch the train back home.

Occasionally he would invite me to join him for drinks in Fleet Street, usually at his favourite pub the Cock Tavern. Occasionally we would visit El Vino's, a rather smart gin palace, where ladies were not allowed at the bar, or the Wig ad Pen Club, frequented as its name suggests by those involved in both the legal system and journalism. There were also the special haunts preferred by the journalists of individual newspapers, such as the Red Lion and the Strachan.

More usually, however, I would take advantage of a

sometimes extended lunch hour to sample the draught Guinness offered by the Irish houses that proliferated in the City then. With office colleagues I would drink pints of the stuff, sometimes laced with mild bitter. Needless to say about this time I ceased to be a stripling, put on about three stone and developed a paunch that I have never completely lost.

I liked and admired Rowney, but his life seemed a waste to me. He was obviously a man of considerable intellectual potential, yet he adopted a pose that was totally anti-culture. He once spent days composing a story for a popular women's magazine of the time, trying to conform to the necessary strict romantic format. His justification? It paid good money! Music of any kind was to him nothing more than a series of noises, with as much creditability, he suggested, as a door slam or a fart. He was delighted when I told him about the emergence of *musique concrete*, claiming this vindicated his views!

He had little time for the visual arts, regarding the work of Picasso, Epstein, Moore and Hepworth with contempt. When it came to prose, however, he was by no means a stick-in-the-mud traditionalist. I managed to get through Joyce's Ulysses with a reasonable degree of understanding, but I stalled at the first page of Finnegans Wake. When I mentioned this to him he claimed he had not only read it, but understood what it was all about! He tried to explain it to me, but without success.

He seemed to regard my interest in the theatre as a youthful aberration, but he did not discourage me providing it did not interfere with my work. I went to the theatre frequently being so fortunate to be living in London. Before it became one of the tourist capitals of the world it was a theatrical paradise. The cost of seats was well within the pocket of a young professional like me. Two of the theatres (then called the New and Wyndhams), operated a system for reserving a seat in the gallery at that night's performance. From 8.0 o'clock in the morning one could book a place in what would that evening become a queue of little numbered stools.

Inevitably my interests turned towards the possibility of writing for the stage. During my studies of Shakespeare and his times I encountered the work of Christopher Marlowe. His life and mysterious early death fascinated me and I tried my hand at writing a play about him. I had learnt from Greek drama that the essential nature of tragedy lay in its inevitability and it seemed to me that Marlowe, by his life and the opinions expressed in his work, had brought his fate upon himself. In "The Death of Christopher Marlowe" I attempted to show that any of its protagonists could have been responsible for the stabbing, which in my play, incidentally, took place in true Greek style, off stage as the final curtain fell!

At that time London had its own "fringe" of small club theatres in Notting Hill Gate, including the Mercury, Watergate, Boltons and New Lindsey. I submitted the play to the Gateway, the director of which was one Olave March. She obviously saw some merit in it, possibly because it had a classical theme and was different from the run-of-the-mill fare she was usually offered. With a little financial help from myself towards the extra costs involved for costumes, etc., she produced it for a two-week run.

Critical response was not enthusiastic, one reviewer suggesting that the dialogue was prosy and that I still had much to learn as a playwright – which was undoubtedly true. In my view the production was not helped by the actor who played Marlowe, who chose to emphasise the playwright's homosexuality. The character of Baines, on the other hand, benefited from a performance of considerable verve by a young Kenneth Haigh, who later made something of a name for himself on television. Perhaps the play would have fared better if he had played the lead.

About this time I was commissioned by Edmonton Borough Council to write a play for a local amateur group as a contribution to the Festival of Britain. I had been reading about the holy thorn that Joseph of Arimathea was reputed to have brought to this country and planted in Glastonbury so devised a plot involving a couple of cockney "spivs" attempting to steal and sell it. Entitled "A Glastonbury Thorn" it was produced at the local town hall. Audiences received it politely, but it failed to make any impact on the theatrical scene.

Chapter 13 - Our theatre in the 50s

The British theatre in the 50s had an astonishing vitality. It was led, of course, by London's West End, which sometimes came in for criticism as being too commercial and unadventurous. Yet it managed to maintain a level of theatrical activity that was the envy of the world and was incidentally nothing short of a miracle in a city that was still recovering from the ravages of a major war.

Theatre owning and production companies run by management dynasties such as Tennent, Albery, Littler, et al, ensured not only that the West End remained open and busy, but its influence spread throughout the country. Productions usually had a pre-London tour, then if successful (or even if not) one that followed the West End run. Once that was over plays could be released for the provincial reps. often waiting eagerly to take advantage of any publicity afforded by the earlier showings.

Much of the fare was run-of-the-mill, but among it were many rare offerings. There was, for example, the attempt to reintroduce poetry into dramatic dialogue. Foremost were the works of Christopher Fry. His period verse drama The Lady's Not for Burning first appeared at the little club theatre known as the Arts and quickly graduated to the West End, where it not only had a popular success, but its title became part of the vernacular. Fry followed it in 1950 by his Venus Observed, with Laurence Olivier in the lead, and then a translation of Ring Round the Moon, by the French dramatist Jean Anouilh. This had a great cast including Paul Scofield (playing a double role), Claire Bloom and Margaret Rutherford. Fry's output included The Firstborn in 1952 and The Dark is Light Enough in 1954. Off-centre, at the Lyric Theatre, in Hammersmith, West London, there was a double bill comprising what many regard as his most enjoyable work: Thor, with Angels, and A Phoenix too Frequent. Once again the playwright was supported by brilliant actors, including Jack Hawkins, Diana Churchill, Dorothy Tutin, a very young George Cole, Jessie Evans in a definitive comedy performance, and, somewhere down the bottom of the cast list, Eric Porter playing A Messenger.

Fry also helped to initiate a movement that it was thought would become an important new feature of British drama – theatre in churches. He wrote a play first produced by the Religious Drama Society at St Thomas's Church, Regent Street. Called A Sleep of Prisoners it was about four prisoners of war interned appropriately enough in a church. Once again Fry's title, with its device of using a singular noun as an adjective describing a group, became a feature of modern parlance, particularly among journalists. The play toured the provinces, usually in churches.

It cannot be said that the concept really took off, however, despite the contribution made by the major poet, TS Eliot. His play Murder in the Cathedral, relating the death of Thomas a'Becket, had its first performance in a church and transferred to the West End, with that great actor Robert Donat in the lead. The atmosphere of the church was missing, however. Also the designer had produced a stage set of solemn grey stone and there were critics who felt Canterbury Cathedral in medieval days would have presented a much more colourful aspect.

Eliot tried to introduce verse dialogue into two modern plays, The Cocktail Party and The Confidential Clerk, but again without a great deal of success, despite the lavish stage settings and star casts. Reviewing them at the time I suggested that neither of them succeeded on either a dramatic, or a poetic level. His dialogue seemed to be filled with watered down poetic clichés and rather embarrassing jokes. His dramatic technique creaked, with the audience on occasion being informed how "crazy" the characters were when, in fact, they were sometimes rather dull..

George Bernard Shaw, who died in 1950 at the age of 94, was still a defining force among those who wanted to see the theatre continue as an important factor in the nation's cultural life. His plays were frequently revived. In 1951 there was a production of Caesar and Cleopatra with a cast of nearly 80, including Laurence Olivier and Vivien Leigh, a financial commitment that would be impossible nowadays for a "straight" play. In February of that year John Clements directed Man and Superman with himself and his wife the lovely Kay Hammond in the leads. This was presented in two versions, the longer one including the "Don Juan in Hell" interlude, making a total running time of four hours. Other Shavian offerings at the time included Pygmalion, once again with John Clements; The Apple Cart, with Noel Coward in the part of King Magnus; You Never Can Tell; and three one-actors under the title "Shavings", demonstrating the breadth of Shaw's dramatic canvas with portraits of Napoleon, Shakespeare and Queen Elizabeth

Writing the famous critical reviews later published collectively in "Our Theatre in the '90s" Shaw had done much to introduce audiences to Ibsen and Tchekov. The Three Sisters was produced in 1951 with Ralph Richardson as Vershinin. There were two productions of The Cherry Orchard, one by the Old Vic Company with Edith Evans heading a prestigious cast, and the other a more humble, but in some ways more satisfying, offering brought to London by the Liverpool Repertory Company, demonstrating the benefits arising in this kind of play from a company of actors performing regularly together.

The influence of Tchekov could be seen in much of the work produced by English dramatists of the day, such as Terence Rattigan, James Brodie, Somerset Maugham, Graham Greene and a lesser-known writer, N. C. Hunter with Waters of the Moon and A Day by the Sea. About this time a precocious young actor named Peter Ustinov, who was to become famous on stage and in film, wrote, directed and appeared in The Love of Four Colonels.

There were many productions of Shakespeare's plays during this period, encouraged and partially financed by the Arts Council. World War 2 was scarcely over when Michael Redgrave produced and starred in Macbeth. During the Festival of Britain Laurence Olivier and Vivien Leigh played in Antony and Cleopatra; John Gielgud was Leontes in The Winter's Tale; Alec Guinness took the lead in his own production of Hamlet, in which he had the novel idea of dressing the cast in Elizabethan costumes. His co-director was Frank Hauser, for whom I later worked during his occupation of the Oxford Playhouse. In 1952 John Gielgud appeared in Much Ado About Nothing, with a cast that included Paul Scofield, Diana Wynyard and Dorothy Tutin. The following year the Shakespeare Memorial Theatre Company in Stratford-upon-Avon, brought their production of Antony and Cleopatra to town with Michael Redgrave, Peggy Ashcroft and Marius Goring in the cast.

Agatha Christie maintained her popularity. The Mousetrap was still in the early stages of its record-breaking run, but she also wrote Witness for the Prosecution, later made into a film. She was deeply loved among the provincial reps, which used to say that in a lean season they only had to present one of her plays to fill the theatre.

During and for a few years after World War 2 the Old Vic Theatre Company was located in what was then called the New Theatre in St Martin's Lane. It moved back to its ancestral home at Waterloo and scores of great classical plays from Shakespeare to Shaw were produced with directors such as Olivier, Tyrone Guthrie, George Devine, Michel Saint-Denis, Glen Byam Shaw. It was with this company that Olivier gave his definitive performance of Richard III. On a comic level that fine character actor Bernard Miles, in the relatively minor part of Christopher Sly, created something of a stir by turning Taming of the Shrew into an opportunity for horseplay. Many neglected masterpieces were revived, such as Jonson's Bartholomew Fair, Marlowe's Dr Faustus and Tamburlaine, Turgenev's A Month in the Country. The great comic actor Miles

Malleson adapted the plays of Moliere, with a modern colloquial text that was not entirely to the liking of some purists

There was also a great deal of theatrical activity on what might be called the periphery of the West End. In the Borough of Kensington the Royal Court Theatre reopened its doors after refurbishment in 1952, with George Devine as its director. In 1956 he established the English Stage Company in order to create what he described as a writers' theatre. He was as good as his word and in that first year John Osborne's Look Back In Anger was produced, initiating the work of those who became known as the angry young men. Osborne followed it with a play entitled The Entertainer, commissioned by and starring Laurence Olivier as Archie Rice. The company continued to present controversial modern plays, such as Eugene Ionesco's The Chairs and The Lesson.

Further west of London in Hammersmith, the Tennent organisation used the Lyric Theatre to try out mainly classical drama such as Shakespeare's Richard II, Tchekov's The Seagull, Congreve's The Way of the World, and Ibsen's A Doll's House. On the other side of the capital and far removed from traditional drama Joan Littlewood was producing new work improvised by herself and her cast. One of the shows that resulted from this was, of course, Oh! What a Lovely War.

Also in east London, at Blackfriars, Bernard Miles established the Mermaid Theatre. Although not intended to be a reproduction of any particular Elizabethan theatre, it was the forerunner of the modern Globe, providing a wide open stage area, where the plays of Shakespeare and his contemporaries could be presented in something resembling the original setting.

Londoners had already enjoyed this form of stage presentation for many years at the Open Air Theatre in Regents Park, albeit on grass. There, during the summer, audiences watched productions that, despite the sometimes intransigent weather, were a delight. The company was led by the redoubtable character actor Robert Atkins. It was agreed that his Bottom was the greatest ever and I remember that his Caliban in The Tempest brought tears to the eyes.

A unique feature of the theatrical scene at that time were the "club" theatres. Mention has already been made of the Notting Hill Gate "fringe", where members could see good quality professional work on a small scale. At the Mercury, for example, I remember Machiavelli's comedy Mandragola; and one of the truly great plays to come out of Ireland, The Playboy of the Western World. In Great Newport Street, just off the Strand, the Arts Theatre Club produced a wide repertoire of plays, classical and modern. It was directed by a fine classical actor Alec Clunes (father of the current television star), appearing as Macbeth and Richard II. The Club's programme included many memorable performances, such Wilfrid Lawson in Strindberg's The Father; Herbert Lomas in Hindle Wakes; Frederick Valk as John Gabriel Borkman; Michael Hordern as Tchekov's Ivanov. At the lower end of the street, nearer the Thames and nestling under railway arches, the Players Club offered theatrical fare of a very different style: Old Thyme Musical Hall with all the trimmings, alliterating master of ceremonies and all!

In addition to the pre- and post- West End tours there were companies that confined themselves to touring, which sometimes involved bringing their shows into peripheral London venues, such as the King's Hammersmith, the Bedford in Camden Town and the People's Palace in the Mile End Road. Best known among these was the company directed by Donald Wolfit, who was virtually the only remaining traditional actor/manager, producing an astonishingly wide repertoire of Shakespeare and other classics.

I recall that when the curtain rose on his production of Julius Caesar he was discovered as Brutus dressed in a white uniform, reclining on a couch centre stage. At the final curtain call for King Lear he would hold on to the drapes, with one hand clutching his chest thanking the audience for helping his company "to bring this great play to life". His acting technique was often criticised for being hammy, but he could also demonstrate a capacity for restraint, and turn in fine under-stated performances when a modern play called for it.

In addition to the traditional and historical drama, the 50s was also a decade of great experimentation in the theatre. There was the existentialism of Jean Paul Satre and Ionesco's theatre of the absurd. James Joyce's former secretary, Samuel Beckett, writing in France (and sometimes in French) produced Waiting for Godot and End Game, which initially was almost denied a licence by the British censor. There was minimalism in the plays of Harold Pinter, who restricted his dialogue to no more than the few words necessary to link his pregnant pauses, something in fact that actors had been doing for generations and still do, regardless of whether the pauses are put in for them or not! Many critics hated this and with the exception of what might be called the intelligentsia, audiences did not initially take to it. Many actors, however, loved it and his plays are now regarded in some circles as classics.

The American influence on the theatre was strong throughout the period. The work of American writers had a vigour and power that was sometimes lacking in the indigenous offerings. Tennessee Williams and Arthur Miller made a particular impact. Their style of writing and scene selection also influenced staging with the use of multiple sets and the new lighting systems. The Method school of acting began to infiltrate this country.

Famous American film stars made their way to the West End to play in roles of their choice. Tyrone Power, one of the biggest names, appeared in the stage version of Mister Roberts at the Coliseum. He was also in a revival of Bernard Shaw's The Devil's Disciple at the Winter Garden. Paul Muni, one of Hollywood's greats, famous for Scarface and The Hunchback of Notre Dame, was the

Salesman who died in Arthur Miller's play. No less a celebrity than Katharine Hepburn played the Millionairess in Bernard Shaw's comedy. Laurence Olivier presented probably the most charismatic Hollywood director and actor of his time, Orson Welles, in a production of Othello, with a young man named Peter Finch playing Iago. For the West End production of A Streetcar named Desire Vivien Leigh reprised her electrifying performance in the film as Blanche, but the only Anglo/American they apparently could find to play Stanley was Bonar Colleano, an excellent actor in his way, but not really able to fill the huge shoes of Marlon Brando.

English actors were greatly in demand in Hollywood. Those who made their names on the London stage were offered majestic salaries to appear in American films, no doubt leading to larger audiences in British theatres when they brought their increased fame back home. Although the cinema was such a major cultural influence its impact on the live theatre was less disastrous than might have been expected. The two cultural forms entered into an uneasy partnership in which there was exchange of dramatic material and casts. The theatre continued to thrive, if a little shakily, alongside its ebullient partner, perhaps because they shared common audiences. People were happy to be leaving home for town and city centres where they could partake of whatever fare was offered, either live on the stage, or flashed on to a screen in a darkened cinema. They might dress up a little more for the theatre, perhaps regarding it as a special occasion. The cinema was something to attend more informally, dressing casually and eating peanuts or sweets during the show

People went to the cinema once, twice, even three times a week, there being plenty of opportunity, particularly in London. The manners, fashions, habits, looks of those they saw on the silver screen affected the way they lived, from smoking as adults to playing cowboys and Indians as children. The great stars, particularly of Hollywood, were idolised, but there was also a great deal of affection for the British cinema. There was also a strong following for films from continental Europe, elite cinemas in London such as The Academy and the Curzon showing films from France, Italy, Poland. We wept at *Jules et Jim* and *Les Enfants du Paradis*. We cried – with laughter – at *M. Hulot's Holiday*.

At this time, however, there was another influence, less benign, slowly raising its relentless head. As children we had first been aware of it when the television mast appeared on the Alexandra Palace. Now the war was over it ceased to be something to be scorned as a novelty. Up to then the only professional entertainment tying us to our fireside was the radio, broadcasting such favourites as Tommy Handley (ITMA) and Arthur Askey as well as the essential news. Now the BBC was helping to develop a form of communication that was to glue the whole population firmly to their living room armchairs and sofas. Television had arrived. Why should we want anything else?

Chapter 14 – Discovering poetry – and love

I had never been drawn strongly towards the writing of, or even reading, poetry. I had read little poetry as a child. Like most boys of my generation I was enthralled by the big five twopenny bloods: Wizard, Adventure, Hotspur, Skipper and Rover, published weekly by D C Thomson and all written – tradition has it – by the same literary genius. I felt stirrings of a poetic muse while at sea. It was difficult not to be moved by the mightiness of the oceans and the exotic nature of my surroundings. My College of the Sea tutor had tried to encourage me, sending me a copy of the Oxford Book of English Verse, which I browsed through, admiring the skill of the poets, but not being quite sure of their purpose. I regarded them with a certain amount of suspicion, not understanding why they should pour forth their emotion in such a contrived way.

When I came ashore my work required me to concentrate on the hard-nosed prose of a journalist, precis writer and sub-editor. One day, however, I sat watching my wife tending the little garden in my old house. It aroused an unusual emotion in me. It was not only the spectacle of the woman I loved enjoying her work. She was undoing some of the hurt and frustration of a childhood in which a locked gate in trellis-work prevented my entry into the tiny floral and grassed area. I wanted to record the moment in words. A prose disquisition did not seem appropriate. Indeed, even now I find it hard to express the incident adequately. Only poetry would suffice and even that could not fully explain the subtlety of my feelings.

The traditional styles I had read came back to me. I wrote a poem in rhyming couplets, described it as a pastiche on 18th century style and entitled it: "On watching a fair gardener tend a dead rose". It began: "Flower your gleam once lit the soil, Tended by a gardener's toil" and ended "Giving the brightest stars to those, who learnt below upon a rose", which may provide an indication of its content and quality. Nevertheless writing a poem was undoubtedly associated with love for my wife.

Later I was to find, like many aspiring poets, that this combination of emotion and creativity often arose from the frustration of unrequited love. My first encounter with frustrated love and the poetry it engendered took place in what would then have been regarded as the unlikely setting of the austere city office in which I worked. Nowadays such activities seem to be almost par for the course! Indeed I have often thought that bringing opposite sexes together in a working environment will, if the geographical conditions allow, almost inevitably result in relationships of this kind. I will not dwell on the details of the affair, which are after all irrelevant to this narrative.

Its impact on my literary development began one day as I stood in the quiet ambience of the local public library, surrounded by the literature of many centuries and diverse nations and felt a euphoria I was unable to explain. The light in that venerable building was filtered through fanlights shrouded partly by green blinds. I had only recently had a tender encounter with my paramour in the office and as I stood in the sober environment I felt the frustration, disappointments, low self-esteem of earlier years fall away from me. I was a man! I was desired, indeed desirable! It must be love. Chairs were not provided in the libraries of those days, but somehow I managed to write on a shorthand notebook some words that expressed the emotions I was feeling.

As the relationship progressed I found myself chronicling it by a sequence of poems which I later entitled: The Discovery of Poetry. It seemed logical to compose them in *vers libre*, which placed me, I suppose, in the respectable company of poets like T. S. Eliot, Ezra Pound and Walt Whitman. There were eight altogether, reflecting the wax and wane of the affair (if that is what it were), and perhaps a few lines from the closing stanza may indicate their quality – or lack of it:

"When in heat of future years
I wander lonely through the flowers dressmakers
Toss out on to summer lawns
Perhaps your spirit
Wandering too
Will set my morsel of remembrance free
And say
You may remember
Though not regain
The happiness that ends with this."

Inevitably after a while the excitement of the situation began to decline, perhaps because of the restrictions placed upon it. A certain boredom crept in and I began to be concerned for its possible impact on my marriage. On her part, however, she appeared to enjoy the opportunities to talk with the young man she obviously regarded as a conquest. It worked its way to its inevitable conclusion. She was engaged and eventually she married. Left to have a baby and returned months later displaying her child proudly as if to say: "look what I have achieved".

For me it was a birth of a different kind. I had discovered poetry and from then on formed the practice of putting my thoughts into verse form. Other aspects of life and the surrounding world inspired me: trees, the London environment, philosophical and humorous ideas, Christmas. Even a spiritual element occasionally intruded into my writing, although I had never been a religious person.

Technically I was particularly exercised by the dichotomy between traditional verse forms and what appeared to be the modern desire of the poetic spirit to break free from them. The use of rhyme as a device was being discredited, alliteration regarded as an historical curiosity. When it came to expressing their deepest emotions, or simply to express ideas to their fellows, however, Shakespeare and his fellow Elizabethans did so through the medium of the sonnet. Nearly 200 years later

Wordsworth revived it in a new, even more profound form. The idea of expressing one's thoughts in a kind of fugal cadence appealed to me.

So I tried my hand at them, deriving intellectual satisfaction from the process. I even translated Ronsard's, where I found a line that predated Herrick by a few years: "Life's roses must be gathered while they may". My French was hardly up to it, but I was amused to reflect that I was following the practice of Ezra Pound, who reckoned he could translate a poem without necessarily knowing the foreign language, something he even applied to Cantonese!

I wanted to write an extended poem – an epic, or at least a narrative. Blank verse was however, also being challenged by modern writers – as it was even in Elizabethan times. Marlowe and the rest found themselves at odds with pedants like Gabriel Harvey, who could not tolerate any deviation from the strict iambic pentameter. Indeed It could be said that Shakespeare was not trying to use the ten-syllable form in his plays, but endeavouring not to! (Try scanning "Howl, howl, howl, Oh! You are men of stone").

In the course of my reading I came across the work of the Troubadours and the later Trouveres, who had such an important influence on the development of English literature, and may be said to have given the world the whole concept of romantic love. Among the stories handed down from that time is that of Serismonda, the heart of whose lover was served up to her in a pie by her jealous husband. It was the tale I was looking for. I set it in a background of the present day, combining the sights and sounds of my beloved London with the exotic environment of Languedoc. I published it many years later, together with some of my other poems, under the title "The Devil and Mrs Brown.

Chapter 15 - Golden days

"Bliss was it in that dawn to be alive, but to be young it was very heaven."

Much has been written and said about the importance of the 60s as a cultural decade. They certainly ushered in the modern world – rock-and-roll, freedom of expression, abstract art, "modern" classical music, the dominance of the flickering domestic screen. But the 50s were for me of greater significance, lit with the colours of a brilliant sunset. The traditional forms of artistic endeavour might have been declining, but they were going out in style.

London in particular enjoyed something of an artistic renaissance after World War 2. The West End theatres had largely survived the blitz and one in particular - the Windmill - claimed it had never closed (or did it mean "clothed"?). Although many of the treasures at the National Gallery were evacuated, it remained open and, like many other similar venues, provided space for concerts throughout and after the war.

Many of the artistic centres in Europe had been devastated, either from the impact of bombardment, or through being occupied by an enemy power. So when European hostilities ended, in addition to its traditional theatrical and musical activities, London became a funnel through which the visual arts of Europe, ancient and modern, passed, were displayed, bought and sold.

As a journalist, working in the centre of the city, living in its near suburbs, I was in a unique position to take advantage of an opportunity to gain an effective, if not exactly academic, education in the subject. London was my tutor, I an eager undergraduate. My work was moderately peripatetic, my lunch hours flexible, my employers tolerant, giving me opportunities to visit art exhibitions, *en passant*. Admission to many of them was either free or of minimal charge. The big prestigious events did not suffer the blight of over-popularity that afflicts many such events today. One did not have to join a queue, or buy a ticket in advance, and once inside one did not find oneself jockeying among the crowds of tourists for a glimpse of the more popular pieces.

I was not encumbered by the use of a car. Indeed, I did not acquire one until I was in my 40s. I travelled by bus and underground, which, in addition to the convenience, provided ample opportunities for supplementing my reading. I remember being involved in Gulliver's Travels on the journey from Wood Green to Leicester Square and being so overwhelmed by the purity of Swift's prose that I went past my station and had to alight at Piccadilly!

Throughout the decade London was awash with exhibits at art galleries, large and small, obviously taking advantage of the movement in works of art that the end of hostilities stimulated. The events fell into two main categories: corporate or officially organised displays; and smaller ones that took place in the showrooms of the many art dealers scattered throughout the West End, and off-centre in such places as Whitechapel and Islington.

One of the most memorable of these was a revelatory exhibition of Picasso's art organised by the Arts Council at the New Burlington Gallery. It comprised work he had produced during his stay in the south of France and was entitled Picasso in Provence. His fame in Britain had been increased by a film entitled "The Picasso Mystery" that had recently been shown at the Curzon Cinema. Those who had seen it, or who knew his work, however, whether admirers or sceptics, could hardly have been prepared for the scene that met them when they entered the Gallery.

It was if the artist had thrown off the restraints and the horrors of the war, exemplified in his great peace painting Guernica, and had indulged himself by creating his own land of light, colour and gaiety. There were paintings in oil and water, drawings and lithographs of a mythical world, with fauns, centaurs and bacchantes, dancing, playing instruments, playing games. But there was more. He had carried this classical theme into a new departure for him, the production of ceramics, spheres and vases, some of which showed the heads of laughing fauns, and others abstract still-lifes and figures.

He had also taken to sculpture, but not the traditional painstaking work in bronze or stone. These were tiny figures of women produced simply with the application of a thumb or stylus on clay. The drawn line of Picasso had always been instantly recognisable as one that could only be produced by the artist and he now seemed to have achieved this "in the round".

When the National and Tate Galleries were fully reopened in 1949 the Arts Council commemorated the event with two major displays from what had recently been enemy countries. In the National Gallery there were over 120 masterpieces from the *Alte Pinakothek*, of Munich, one of the world's greatest art collections. The Tate held a major exhibition of works from Vienna, including not only paintings and sculpture in bronze, wood and stone, but also Greek and Roman antiquities, tapestries, jewellery, arms and armour, manuscripts and astronomical instruments and clocks.

The Arts Council ensured that the work of past great English artists was not neglected and those of the present day were also given adequate wall space. The stately figures and landscapes of the 18th century were represented in major exhibitions of William Hogarth and Thomas Gainsborough. There were watercolours and drawings of the same period by the more frivolous Thomas Rowlands. Two anthologies of the work of modern British painters were held in 1951, introducing the public to the works of many artists who have since become household names, such as Francis Bacon, Edward Burra, Lucien Freud, Ivor Hitchens, L. S. Lowry, Wyndham Lewis, Paul Nash, Ben Nicholson, John Piper, Matthew Smith, Stanley Spencer, Graham Sunderland, to mention but a few.

Every year the Royal Academy would mount its annual exhibition to a chorus of criticism from the cognoscenti on what they regarded as the unadventurous and traditional form many of the exhibits took. They seemed to overlook, however, that this was the annual show of a teaching academy and the works on display were mainly the first steps of art students. The Academy also held major exhibitions of European art, in particular one displaying Landscape in French Art from Claude and Poussin of the 17th century to Degas and Seurat of the 20th. An exhibition of works produced in the first half of the 20th century entitled *L'Ecole de Paris* demonstrated that French Impressionism and Post-Impressionism lasted well into this period, with many of its best known practitioners still alive: Utrillo had not yet succumbed to drink. Henri Matisse was still active, as were Georges Braque, Max Ernst, Marc Chagall and Raoul Dufy.

The Academy also brought major exhibitions of Dutch paintings to London. In 1950-51 there were works by Holbein and other masters of the 16th and 17th centuries; and in 1952-53 Dutch pictures of three centuries from 1450-1750. For some reason this was combined with an exhibition of paintings by 16th century Italian artists, whose work was so severely criticised by Ruskin and other 19th century commentators. At this time, too, the Academy organised a Leonardo da Vinci quincentenary exhibition, which included a selection of some of the finest of the artist's drawings from the royal collection.

These exhibitions represented the official face of artistic activity. In addition there was a plethora of private showrooms, small and large, through which it seemed the art of the world was passing from seller to buyer. There were also small specialist exhibitions supported by sponsors with a particular interest in their subject. The casual visitor could attend, pick up a catalogue and view the works on display with no greater responsibility than a pleasant greeting to the attendant.

In the course of little more than a month, for example, a major loan exhibition of works by Rubens was held at the Wilderstein Gallery under the auspices of the Royal

Empire Society and in aid of The Lord Major's National Thanksgiving Fund. Then Thomas Agnew and Sons, Ltd, mounted a centenary loan exhibition of water-colour drawings by Turner in aid of the Artists General Benevolent Institution; the Matthiessen Gallery had an exhibition of French Master Drawings of the 18th Century for the benefit of the French Hospital in London.

Roland, Browse and Delbanco showed one of the few exhibitions of that fine British impressionist, Sickert, although one was also held during Festival year in the public library at Islington, where he lived and worked for many years. At the Lefevre the stick-like figures of L. S. Lowry could be seen, recent sculpture and drawings of Barbara Hepworth and for the first time the mobiles of Alexander Calder. Arthur Tooth and Sons Ltd could proudly announce a collection of pictures recently purchased in France, including the work of Renoir, Boudin, Courbet, Camille Pissarro, Monet, Corot, Cezanne. The Matthiesen had a particularly fine selection of the work of Pissarro. The Marlborough held a whole series of exhibitions of work by French masters of the 19th and 20th centuries, again containing many fine paintings by such artists as Renoir, Sisley, Monet, Modigliani and, one recalls, a very early uncharacteristically impressionist work by Picasso.

The work of young unknown British artists was promoted in several small galleries, such as Gimpel Fils. The Leicester had a show entitled "Artists of Fame and of Promise". At the Hanover there were paintings by Graham Sutherland. The New Burlington Galleries showed the work of the so-called London Group. Art was kept alive in London's far East End by The Whitechapel Art Gallery, which annually showed painting and sculpture by people who lived and worked in the area. During Festival year it held an exhibition entitled Black Eyes and Lemonade, containing an extraordinary range of British popular and traditional art, from Staffordshire pottery to toys, games and foodstuffs.

In 1950 there was an exhibition of modern art at the Tate, including a semi-abstract "single form of continuity in space" by Boccioni; and a relief of the Crufixion by Manzu. Paintings in this event included the surrealist landscapes of de Chirico and characteristic works by the wonderful Modigliani. About this time the Arts Council organised an exhibition of Mexican Art, providing a unique insight into the culture of that country. Other international art on show included Chinese ceramics from the collection of Alan Barlow; and French Paintings of the 19th Century from that of William Burrell. Imported from the *Musee d'Art Moderne*, in Paris.

In 1952 the Arts Council organised, in association with the Congress for Cultural Freedom, an exhibition of 20th Century masterpieces, including works as diverse as that of the "primitive" Henri Rousseau, the American sculptor Caldwell, such abstract painters as Juan Gris, George Braque, Joan Miro and Picasso, the Italian Futurists, and later French impressionists, including Pierre Bonnard, Raoul Dufy, Georges Seurat and Henri Matisse. Edvard Munch's Scream became part of popular culture through the medium of the cinema, but it was first introduced to the general British public in an exhibition of his work organised by the Arts Council in 1951, although it was then called The Cry.

One event above all others typified this cultural upsurge and lifted the spirits of a whole nation after the greyness and tragedy of the War. In 1947 the then Labour government decided to commemorate the centenary of the great 1851 exhibition with what became known as the Festival of Britain. The proposal was greeted as an absurd waste of money by many and when the project became a reality there were those who found much to criticise and even condemn. Most of my generation, however, saw it as a symbol of a better, brighter future, a tremendous act of faith.

It is difficult to communicate the sense of euphoria the event created for those who had lived through the exigencies of life in war-torn London. It was a challenge to the powers of darkness, a festival of light, gaiety, of the human spirit trying to shake off the horrors of war. On the South Bank the Skylon pointed the way to the stars; the Dome of Discovery was balanced like a ballet dancer on delicate legs; dismal railway arches suddenly blossomed with painted colour; flights of stairs were designed so that ascending them was actually pleasurable.

Works of art and design were especially commissioned. One could see sculpture by Henry Moore, Lynn Chadwick, Jacob Epstein, Barbara Hepworth, Reg Butler; there were murals in paint and ceramics from Laurence Scarfe, Victor Pasmore, Feliks Topolski and John Piper. We were fortunate in the weather and we danced under the lights and the stars on the Promenade. No doubt my personal sense of a nation reborn was partly due to the fact that when my wife and I danced under the lights of the Promenade she was pregnant!

The pleasures of the Festival were not restricted to the South Bank, however. Further up river in Battersea Park art and entertainment merged. On the one hand there were the so-called Pleasure Gardens, which did their best to combine a fun fair of superior proportions with the more stately traditions associated with the Vauxhall of an earlier age. Once again designers of genius were employed to make this an unforgettable experience for people of all ages. The principal architects of the Grand Design were John Piper and Osbert Lancaster and, at the other end of the scale, Emmett, with his Far Tottering and Oyster Creek Railway.

Then there was the Mermaid with Two Tails, sculptured in bronze by Arthur Fleischmann; a Fountain Tower topped by a lighted pineapple; and the amazing Guinness clock. The Gardens even had their own theatres: the Riverside, where Andrew Sachs introduced the Victorian "Late Joys" music hall that had started life at the Players Theatre. In a venue called the Amphitheatre Lupino Lane, the scion of a famous theatrical family dating back three centuries, presented his cockney entertainment of Pearly Kings and Queens, all buttons, bows and feathers.

More serious artistic stimulation was provided by an open air exhibition of sculpture, organised jointly by the Arts Council and what was then London County Council. The first such event had been held in 1948, when it was a great success and the Festival provided an opportunity to repeat it. Viewers were reminded that the true place of sculpture was not in a museum or attached to a building, but standing outside, on its own, in congenial surroundings.

This concept had been initiated by Jacob Epstein, a highly controversial figure, whose piece entitled Rima located in Hyde Park had created so much animosity that paint was thrown over it. Another work to cause a stir was his stone rendering of Lazarus. A much better indication of this artist's genius and the breadth and sensitivity of his work, however, was provided the following year in an Arts Council's exhibition. It included, for example, the exquisite carving of Two Doves, the extraordinary figure of a pregnant woman entitled Genesis and many busts of well-known figures of the day, including Einstein, Bernard Shaw, Pandit Nehru and Ralph Vaughan Williams.

Henry Moore contributed work to both Battersea and the South Bank itself and to coincide with the Festival, the Arts Council organised a major exhibition of his work at the Tate Gallery, comprising not only many of his monumental sculptures in stone and bronze, but also drawings, some of which were from the series he produced of sleepers in the London underground stations during the blitz.

There were several pieces in the park by Barbara Hepworth, then beginning to make her mark, and there was work by other abstract artists who were being increasingly recognised, such as Reg Butler, Nicolas Pevsner and Ossip Zadkine. More traditional sculptors were also represented, with a bronze of Orpheus by Rodin, and a bronzed plaster cast called "Mediterranean 1901" by

Maillol. Eric Gill, who is perhaps better known for the sans serif typefaces, showed a striking piece in black stone

There were also many examples of sculpture from abroad, Italy's Manzu and Marini: Wotruba and Soukop, from Vienna; Vogel, from Bohemia; Nimptsch, Henghes and Kolby from Germany; Pompon, of France; the spindly figures of the Swiss Giacometti stood pointing at the American Calder's hanging "mobiles", which were regarded as sculpture, but were rapidly becoming a design cliché, suspended over the cots of many an infant.

This interest in sculpture continued and developed after the Festival. In 1954 the Arts Council arranged another open air exhibition, this time in Holland Park. It contained only 30 pieces, but all of a very high quality, including one of the few pieces of sculpture produced by Renoir. On a smaller scale, it set up a number of exhibitions entitled "Sculpture in the Home", showing works that might be regarded as suitable for domestic display by both famous and lesser-known artists, although it is doubtful if many of those attending the exhibitions would be able to afford an Epstein bust or a Henry Moore reclining figure!

An outcome from the Festival that was perhaps less satisfying aesthetically was the surrounding development that became known as the South Bank. The stairs in the Festival itself might have been pleasurable, but those that surrounded the area were in heavy concrete as were the grey buildings they served. It was at the beginning of gigantism in architecture, where the design mattered more than the impact on those who used it, where human beings would have to travel in metal cages up to the tops of high rise buildings, far from grass and trees and flowers and devoid even of the warmth of humanity.

Doubts were raised about the design of the Festival Hall, which we were given to understand had been built "from the inside out", but in fulfilment resembled nothing more an aircraft hangar. It was years before those responsible could be persuaded to pierce its aggressive façade with the windows of a restaurant, allowing people to look out at the river and the passing humanity.

So I was able to imbibe a level of artistic activity that has probably seldom been equalled. It was a wonderland, a stage performance acted out over the historic streets of London. Nowadays I frequently dream I am wandering in the streets of an unidentified city in which the locations are only partially recognisable as London. It is a longing, I suppose, for those far-off days. It is the pantomime of my childhood. I wake up in the adult equivalent of tears, knowing it will never happen again.

Chapter 16 – Give me excess of it

In the 21st century, although the works of Beethoven, Mozart, et al, are still revered and played, when the younger generation in particular talk about "music" they are usually referring to what is known as pop, or rock. In the 1950s "music" would generally mean that produced by symphony orchestras, "chamber" groups, classical soloists and the like. "Popular" music was accepted, providing it was in a recognisable format and confined to dance halls and cinemas.

As children in the 30s and 40s we certainly preferred that kind of music, but it usually reached our ears only from mechanical sources, like the radio. This took the form of a single wooden box in the living room, shared with adults. As youngsters we preferred to gather round the scratchy turntables of wind-up gramophones, enchanted by the recordings of songs many of which we heard for the first time in films.

Music was one of the many ways cinema influenced our young lives. A little girl won our hearts skipping down a yellow brick road with a voice so distinctive and beguiling that a single phrase could be instantly recognisable. Bing Crosby, a short, balding man with over-large ears and a wry sense of humour, crooned his way into our affections, particularly when he was paired with comedian Bob Hope, who could also turn out a tuneful vocal when called upon. Fred Astaire, a thin dancer with an aquiline nose and unimpressive physique, achieved fame (particularly in his partnership with Ginger Rogers) as a romantic hero by a combination of terpsichorean skills and a total belief in his infallibility as a lover. The plots were often nonsensical, the dialogue trite, but the love interest came magically alive not in what the characters said or acted, but in their dance.

To Bing Crosby and Fred Astaire can be added others such as Frank Sinatra (the first truly mass pop idol) and

Gene Kelly, who brought a degree of balletic respectability to ballroom and tap. The technique all these singers used was known as crooning dependant on the microphone to amplify voices that would not otherwise have been heard beyond the front row of the stalls. The songs they sang were not regarded as having any lasting aesthetic value, although many of them have not only retained their popularity, but are now considered by many as holding their own with such classical composers as Schubert and Schuman. Composers like Irving Berlin, Cole Porter, Hoagy Carmichael, George and Ira Gershwin competed with one another to produce memorable songs for film and solo artist.

With the emergence of what became known as "swing" a whole new musical industry was born. Nowadays it is known as "big band" to distinguish it from jazz, out of which it grew and with which it is sometimes confused. In my view the two use totally different techniques. Jazz comprises improvisation on a basic theme by individual members of a small group. The music of swing was closely arranged, with occasional "riffs", or solos by individual musicians. .Jazz never greatly appealed to me. There was a jazz club at 100 Oxford Street, which I occasionally visited, but it seemed somewhat esoteric and became increasingly so.

We all loved the American musicians who formed their own orchestras and headed them with their instrumental speciality: Benny Goodman, Woody Hermann and Artie Shaw on clarinet; the Dorsey brothers, Tommy and Jimmy on saxophone and trombone (I can't remember which was which!); Harry James on trumpet; and Louis Armstrong not only playing an electrifying trumpet, but also singing in his characteristic style. Then there were Duke Ellington and Count Basie leading their orchestras from the piano.

One of the finest exponents was Glen Miller, the sound of whose music was very distinctive. Unlike his peers he did not play an instrument, but conducted from the front in traditional style. His orchestra featured in a film, he and other instrumentalists playing parts. Another film about his band starred James Stewart playing Glen. His music was greatly loved by us and there was universal sadness at his premature death in a plane crash.

There were many British bands that were respected and admired, but did not for us achieve the glamour of their American counterparts. We listened to Geraldo, Ambrose, Oscar Rabin and the like on the gramophone, went to their concerts, usually held on Sundays at local cinemas, and danced to them or their imitators at the numerous ballrooms, but we reserved our full enthusiasm for the trans-Atlantic sounds

One day an "art" film appeared that had a big impact musically on us young people. Produced by the Disney studio and called Fantasia, it was shown initially in a small cinema in Tottenham Court Road. People queued for hours to see and hear it, but there were those who found its presentation of potted classics superficial and poorly interpreted. Lovers of Beethoven threw up their hands in horror at the Pastoral Symphony being presented as a kind of playground for mythical characters. Many felt that abstract patterns did nothing to add to the greatness of Bach's Staccato and Fugue, although to me they seemed particularly apt. They hated it when Mickey Mouse appeared on the podium to pull at Stokowski's coat tails. Disney had done something unforgivable: he had popularised classical music. But for us it was magical. We watched, loved and talked about it, even humming snatches of the music while we sat on our bikes by the side of a boating lake in the local park.

So as young teenagers we began to develop an ambivalent attitude towards classical music. The relationship was probably not far different from that existing today between pop and symphony. Of the great American song-writers only Gershwin bridged the gap between the two disciplines with such works as Rhapsody in Blue and – even more remarkably – the opera Porgy and Bess.

Nowadays, f a young person is interested in music he or she would pick up a guitar and begin to play. Then they were confined to the popular music of Spain or South America. There was a minor interest in the classical guitar, the only well-known exponent of which was, of course, Segovia. To most of us domestic music was played on the piano and it saddens me to this day that I was never given the opportunity to play on the one in our living room. One of my friends did achieve a degree of skill on the instrument. His family was sufficiently well-off to be able to afford two grand pianos in the living room of their house in the up-market neighbouring borough of Palmers Green, where we would gather to hear him play.

He had a sister, who was beautiful, tall and blonde. She swam and ice-skated and was regarded by all of us as something of a star. She developed a fondness for one of our group with the surname Rose, a Jewish lad, who although short and dark was equally athletic and popular. They became engaged to be married and for reasons that were not clear to us at the time her mother took great exception to the relationship.

One day when we were gathered to hear my friend play, I was persuaded to sing with him. I had been having voice production lessons and had a small repertoire. The piece that suited my voice best was "The English Rose". I started to sing and suddenly the girl's mother saw the funny side of it. She started to call out "English Rose, English Rose!" and laughed uncontrollably, eventually becoming hysterical and rushing from the room. I later learned that when the young couple eventually did marry she cut up her daughter's wedding clothes.

Classical music events proliferated. The Promenade Concerts at the Royal Albert Hall were inspirational, particularly those on Friday given up entirely to the works of Beethoven. One stood in the downstairs arena, or wandered around the balcony of the huge building, hearing the finest symphony orchestras and the most celebrated conductors and soloists. The Royal Philharmonic, presided over by that bearded tyrant, Thomas Beecham, was regarded as among the best. Then there was the BBC Symphony, the London Symphony, the Philharmonia and, of course, from Manchester the Halle, under the great John Barborolli. Other conductors frequently on the podium were the much loved Adrian Boult and Malcolm Sargeant, who for some reason was unkindly referred to as "flash Harry" and I believe still is!

The Royal Festival Hall eventually became available for concerts, although the acoustics came in for much criticism. Having endured the booming echoes of the Albert Hall for many years music lovers now found the keen purity of the new building even less to their liking. It is interesting that, although the first concert at the new Festival Hall comprised works by English composers, despite the fact that the War had ended only a few years previously the following one was all Beethoven. Other German composers featured fully in the remainder of the concerts, demonstrating the power of music to overcome prejudice and cross national barriers.

Great orchestras of the world visited London. I recall a series of concerts by the Philadelphia Orchestra under its pint-sized conductor Eugene Ormandy; and the Vienna Philharmonic playing Beethoven's 9th, with Wilhelm Furtwangler achieving his most stunning affects by throwing his vast bald dome of a head at the players! There were those, however, who found a rather more muted performance by our own Adrian Boult more to their liking.

There was a great deal of innovation in classical music, not all of it appreciated by the aficionados. Shostakovich was regarded as "modern", but there was no doubt about the positive impact of his fifth symphony when it was played for the first time at a promenade concert. We weren't too sure what to make of William Walton, but we had no trouble with Vaughan Williams, particularly his London Symphony. We accepted what Debussy was doing with the pentatonic scale, but the music of Stravinsky and

Bartok was cacophonic in ways we could not always understand.

There was a movement away from the vast choral concerts traditionally associated with Bach and Handel. Older musical instruments such as the harpsichord were introduced and about this time The Galpin Society organised an exhibition of relics, including a selection of flageolets, cornets, serpents, virginals, harpsichords and clavichords, as well as such rarities as a gittern, a cittern, harp-lute and symphonium.

Once a year, on Palm Sunday, the Bach Choir with the Jacques Orchestra under its inspirational conductor Reginald Jacques would present Bach's St Matthew Passion, in its entirety, at the Royal Albert Hall. Jacques believed that the smaller size of both orchestra and choir more closely provided the kind of sound that Bach would have expected, and this effect was augmented by the introduction of a harpsichord as well as an organ for the continuo. The concerts were held in two parts with an interval providing an opportunity for picnic lunch in Hyde Park.

Opportunities to hear good music were not confined to the large concert halls. While I was working in the City of London it was frequently possible to hear small-scale musical offerings in local halls and churches, often on the organ. There was even a course of evening classes in "musical appreciation" held at the City Literary Institute., where a tutor would play pieces from the classical repertoire on a gramophone and analyse them.

I particularly remember the lunch-time concerts presented by the City Music Society at the nearby Bishopsgate Institute or the Mermaid Theatre. There one could partake of a sandwich and a cup of coffee and settle down to listen to the piano works of Chopin or Listz; a string trio, or a quartet; and a young Julian Bream on the guitar.

At one lunch-time concert there was a performance by an astonishing new phenomenon. A male singer appeared and sang on the soprano stave. He was Alfred Deller, first of the counter tenors. (A comment could clearly be heard among the audience: "No dear, he's not castrati.") I am not an expert, but I believe the technique is that of a baritone, using only half the vocal chords, like the G & S patter singer. I am reminded, too, of the lover in the Shakespeare play, who "doth sing both high and low".

Following the impact of Fantasia, the popularising of classical music continued. In Harringay, North London, there was a vast arena for ice skating, ice hockey and speedway racing. In the late 40s and early 50s, a group of impresarios had the idea of presenting "concerts for the people", attracting audiences in the tens of thousands to hear the more popular pieces in the classical music genre. Those taking part included such celebrities as Yehudi Menuhin, conductor/pianist Jose Iturbi, and an amazing child prodigy, ten-year-old Pierino Gamba.

Sadly there came a time when the Arena was sold to make way for more commercial enterprises. What had been a wonderful focus for community activities closed without any regard for the gap it left in the lives of all, young and old. Later the borough of Haringay itself was merged with Wood Green and Tottenham to form a monstrosity called Haringey - a name that could only have been conjured up by a committee of civil servants!

For many people, of course, the most enjoyable way to hear music is on the stage and for them the London theatre in those days was Utopia. Many large theatres had thankfully avoided the ravages of the blitz. Seat prices, not yet inflated by the impact of tourism, were easily affordable by all but the most penurious. At Covent Garden operatic offerings ranged from Mozart to Richard Strauss; and there were novelties such as Henry Purcell's The Fairy Queen and Benjamin Britten's Gloriana. Laurence Olivier presented Gian-Carlo Menotti's opera The Consul. Elsewhere in London there was a production of George Gershwin's opera, Porgy and Bess.

Sadler's Wells, a delightful theatre in Islington that had

reopened in the 30s, offered an interesting programme of opera and ballet, including some works that are less frequently seen, such as Gounod's Faust, Rossini's La Cenerencola, Saint-Saens' Samson and Delilah, as well as better known works by Mozart, including The Marriage of Figaro and both versions of Il Seraglio.

One could hear Purcell's Dido and Aeneas at the Mermaid, Flecker's Hassan with Delius's music at the Cambridge and Sheridan's The Duenna at the Westminster. At the little Fortune Theatre the Intimate Opera Society presented such novelties as The Musick Master, by Pergolesi; True Blue, or The Press Gang, a musical interlude by Henry Carey; Don Quixote, with music by Purcell; Bach's Coffee Cantata; and The Musical Courtship, a comic dialogue written by James Hook.

Ballet was not a principal interest of mine, but I did not miss the opportunity to see Margot Fonteyn, Nadia Nerina and others at the Royal Opera, as well as Moira Shearer, who did much to popularise the art form through her performance in the film of the Red Shoes. A number of international dance companies visited London. One calling itself Choreographic Productions Ltd presented International Ballet at the Coliseum and London Casino. Antonio brought his Spanish ballet to the Stoll; Ram Gopal his Indian Dancers and Musicians to the Adelphi; Jose Greco electrified audiences at the Royal Festival Hall with his Spanish dancing; and the Dancers of Bali appeared at the Winter Garden Theatre "with full gamelan orchestra".

For those with lighter tastes in music what used to be known as "musical comedy" maintained its popularity and was about to undergo a sea change. Composers like Ivor Novello had dominated the genre for years, producing tuneful works that differed from grand opera in particular by the inclusion of spoken dialogue instead of recitative. Gilbert and Sullivan seemed to suffer something of a decline during the period, but there were many performances of what might be described as the European tradition.

I can remember a delightful performance of The Merry Widow at Sadler Wells, with June Bronhill in the lead. She was also scintillating in Orpheus in the Underworld, performing one of her arias in a bath clad apparently in nothing but bubbles! In a London suburb at the Finsbury Park Empire, I saw John Hanson, a popular tenor of the time, playing the lead in Sigmond Romberg's The Student Prince He impressed audiences not only for his fine voice, but also his singularly dark and luxurious hair-piece! These shows were unashamedly sentimental. The curtain would rise on a chorus and close with the leading actors going off into the sunset.

After World War 2, however, significant changes were introduced from across the Atlantic. "Musical comedy" became "the musical". Plots became more realistic and even serious. When the curtain went up for the first time on Oklahoma a startled West End audience was treated not to the traditional line up of singing and dancing ladies and gentlemen, but a single baritone declaiming: "Oh! what a beautiful morning". Here were not the dukes and duchesses, diplomats and ladies of fashion in their elegant settings, but cowboys and cowgirls, in the barns and prairies of America's mid-west. The themes of later offerings were even more innovative: Carousel set in a fair ground; South Pacific among the GIs of an island military base; modern versions of Shakespeare with Kiss Me Kate and West Side Story; stories adapted from other English literary backgrounds, such as The King and I, My Fair Lady and Cabaret. In more modern times this tendency has become even darker and deeper, with Sweeny Todd, Phantom of the Opera, Les Miserables and others.

I cannot leave my account of musical life in the mid-20th century without mentioning a form of music that almost passed me by and indeed would have escaped me completely were it not for my wife.. This was the brass band. I had spent most of my life in the south of England and knew little of traditions in the north. There were brass bands elsewhere, but in the coal-mining areas of such counties as Durham and Northumberland it was an integral part of cultural life. My wife's father, Stan Parker, played the trumpet. He was a professional musician still playing in a variety theatre in Gateshead and obviously much sought after by local amateur brass bands, with which he played regularly.

Every year those who worked in the mines of England's north east held what was known as the Durham Miners Gala, organised by the relevant trade union. My wife and I were invited to join them. We stayed overnight at her former house in a suburb of Gateshead known as Low Fell and got up early next morning to catch a train at the local station.

After all these years it comes to my mind almost as a television documentary. The early morning light shines on the rows of terrace houses. There are few people about and, of course, few cars to be seen, if any. Along the empty streets isolated figures pass, some of them carrying an instrument. At the station a few others are waiting. When the train arrives more musicians are on board from further up the line. The next station is more crowded and there is much good-hearted jostling and joking as they join us. The rivulets join as a stream.

When the train arrives at its destination, Durham, it disgorges its load and we realise how great the numbers are. The stream has become a river. Each band has a leader, a drum major. They leave the station and begin to march. They are joined by others coming from different directions. The streets are narrow and from between the leaning buildings of the old town further rivers of humanity appear to join the main procession.

The bands play, not in any organised fashion, but giving a joyful sound. When they reach the town centre they fall silent and wait to receive the salute from the Town Hall balcony by the year's guest, Aneurin Bevan. Having paid their respects, the vast flood, which started as a few rain drops from so many different parts of the county, move on to the race course, where they join together to celebrate in a great sea of souls.

One day I opened my copy of The Daily Telegraph and was surprised to read the review of a concert not by the BBC Symphony Orchestra, or a great pianist, but a group calling itself The Beatles. It was some time before I realised that the name did not relate to insects, but to "les beats". Rock and roll had arrived. It was the end of the 1950s and although we did not realise it at the time, it was also the end of what may be regarded as the classical era. A new decade ushered in a new world, one to which I personally would never completely relate. Fortunately, it would not concern me as I had a new and exciting career to begin.

Chapter 17 – An actor's life for me

I have expanded at length on my early life and the cultural environment of the 1950s not only because it had such an important impact on my development, but also in the hope it may serve as an historic record of the period before social and artistic life changed on so many different levels from the early 60s onwards. If readers have been patient enough to remain with my narrative so far, they may be relieved to find that I have at last reached the part that relates to the main theme.

One day I learnt that there was a vacancy for a part-time assistant stage manager in a local weekly repertory theatre known as the Intimate in the neighbouring borough of Palmers Green. This had been established in the 1930s by John Clements, who later became a major film and stage star. It was in a converted church hall, small and suffering from having no rake in its single-level auditorium, so that those in the back rows had a restricted view of the stage. The constraints of weekly programme changes placed a strain both on stage and behind it and there were those who said unkindly that audiences only went there to enjoy the occasional "dry" by the actors, mishaps with the scenery, or mislaid properties.

Nevertheless it was popular and well attended by a regular clientele, enjoying the performances of a resident company and the occasional guest artiste. Because of its proximity to Central London the little theatre was able to attract many fine actors in the early stages of their careers, who welcomed the opportunity to gain experience and perhaps invite agents and producers to watch them perform.

Most important for me it was professional and could be the first step on a golden ladder. I would work in tandem with the present ASM, who was also part-time. During the day we would share responsibility for attending rehearsals, which were held in central London. I would have to attend performances every evening with a matinee on Thursdays, and dress rehearsals on Monday afternoons. It would pay a pittance! My work as a journalist was not to them a hindrance, but how would it be received at the Mercantile Guardian?

Needless to say, Rowney's reaction was typical. He asked me if I thought I could complete my duties for the MG in half a day. I said I could and he agreed to the arrangement. It seemed to work well. Rehearsals were held in one of the many studios existing in the backstreets of Soho. My co-ASM ran them in the mornings and I joined them for the afternoon. After rehearsals I would make my way home for a meal before attending at the theatre to get ready for the evening performance.

The director, Peter Coleman, was a dear man, with a very sweet temperament. He was tolerant of our backstage arrangement, providing everything worked professionally. Sadly, he had an addiction to alcohol that eventually took control of his life. He was a brilliant actor and idolised another great character actor with a similar problem, Wilfred Lawson. Years later I learned Peter's career ended when he collapsed on stage during a performance. Inevitably, he died from his affliction.

I had managed to initiate myself into the professional theatre, albeit in the humblest way. The trouble was I had no training, had not attended RADA, or LAMDA. Had not enjoyed the advantages of a drama society at university. Was not fortunate enough to be part of the great acting fraternities, such as the Redgraves, or the Mills. It would be difficult for me to earn a living and support a family on the occasional opportunities offered to an inexperienced actor. It was obviously going to be necessary to combine acting with stage management and directorial skills.

I never had any doubt, however that this was my chosen profession. One night I was alone in the theatre after everyone else had left. I went on to the stage, gazed out at the empty auditorium and thought: "I have come home. Here I can do anything." And I could! I had always been somewhat introspective, battling with an inferiority complex, but standing on that stage, in that small grubby theatre I felt in command, of myself and my surroundings.

My first professional appearance on stage was in a play called Dear Charles that had had a successful West End run with a famous character actress named Yvonne Arnaud. It was there I had my first lessons in stage technique. The female "juvenile" lead was Vivienne Merchant, who later married Harold Pinter and achieved recognition as a fine actress in her own right. I was to play her fiancé, appearing only briefly. I had merely to shake the hand of the protagonist and respond to her welcoming comments. Then Vivienne took me upstage to look out of French windows. As we stood there she muttered under her breath: "wake up". I realised what was expected of me and "came alive". She taught me how to achieve this on stage even when one was not immediately involved in the action.

Vivienne had another important influence on my theatre work. She urged me to have my voice trained, not only so that I could be heard in a theatre auditorium, but also to remove any traces of a cockney accent – except, of course, when it was required for a part! I was obviously not in a position to attend an acting school, such as RADA and anyway the idea of doing so did not appeal. It had a reputation for producing students with a stylised technique and a big booming voice considered appropriate for Shakespeare, but not necessarily for the sort of work I would be involved in.

I answered an advertisement in the local newspaper offering voice production lessons. It had appeared there for many years under the name Leslie Irons so that I expected to be met by an elderly man when arrived at his home and was surprised to be welcomed by someone of my own age. He explained that he had succeeded to the practice on the death of his father, who had the same name and had been a voice teacher and choir leader.

He suggested that if I wished to develop my voice for

speaking I might as well learn to sing at the same time. Having been discouraged when I was a boy I told him firmly that I could not sing, but he insisted that anyone could do so, unless they were tone deaf. It was a matter, he suggested, not of learning something, but unlearning personal and environmental restraints. He played a note on the piano and I emitted something that might have been produced by a pig being stuck.

Leslie was a Christian Scientist and, although I could never accept the principles of his beliefs, I found his concepts of contemplation and "mind-over-matter" greatly helped in overcoming my restrictive complexes. Together we went on to develop my light tenor voice that was not only of use to me on stage, but has remained with me in later years when choral singing became one of my most enjoyable recreations.

Another popular member of the Intimate cast and a great favourite with audiences was a talented comic actor named Ray Dyer. He also fancied himself as a playwright and during my stay at the theatre produced two murder mysteries: Wanted One Body and Time Murderer Please. Those of us who worked backstage thought they were terrible and would cringe with embarrassment at what we felt was a poor audience response.

Many years later I went to see a play that had received critical acclaim at the Wyndhams Theatre in the West End. It was called "Rattle of a Simple Man". Virtually a two-hander, it starred that great comic actress Sheila Hancock and a young actor later to become well known to television viewers, Edward Woodward. The author was someone called Charles Dyer and when I looked at his photograph in the programme I found that he was in fact Ray. Later he achieved a similar success with a play called "The Staircase", depicting two homosexual hairdressers, one of whom was played by that great classical actor Paul Schofield. I have often wondered how the transformation took place from a writer of heavily plotted pot-boilers to what were intellectual conversation pieces.

I enjoyed my work at the Intimate, but an even more exciting opportunity arose to work in a theatre on the other side of London. This was the New Lindsey, one of the Notting Hill clubs. It was being run by two young Oxbridge graduates, who were offering an interesting programme of plays. Once again I was able to negotiate a sharing situation with my editor and at the theatre took on the dual role of stage managing and acting. I was answerable to a wondrously plump stage director named Peggy Ann Clifford, who seemed able despite her cumbersome figure to negotiate the cramped space backstage with an almost balletic grace.

It appeared that my work as stage manager included that of electrician, something about which I then had little experience or even knowledge. After all, I had been brought up – and still lived – in a home lit by gas and candles. One day the theatre received a visit from a local authority inspector to check safety aspects. He managed to obtain a positive electrical reading from a radiator and told me that unless something was done about the wiring the place would be closed. There was nothing else for it. Somehow I had to set to and practically rewired the building!

The producers revived a little-known play by John Masefield called "The Witch", set in medieval times. The casting called for two soldiers. I was cast as one, but it was felt the budget would not run to another actor, so I had to play both. At one point in the play they were positioned on opposite sides of the stage. I had to enter from prompt corner as one soldier and cross the stage in order to play the other. To make this plausible I had to draw attention to a trail of blood on the scenery, crying "There's blood on the walls, and there, and there". I used to rehearse this at home, using all the volume that my voice lessons had developed. One day there was a hammering on the front door of my house. The police had been called by an anxious neighbour.

To cope with this double work load it was necessary to

arrive early in the morning at the Mercantile Guardian office, sometimes before seven o'clock. By midday I had completed the necessary editorial tasks and would catch a number 25 bus across London, on which I would eat sandwiches for my lunch. At the theatre I participated in the afternoon rehearsals, then set up the stage for the evening performance, running the "corner", working the "electrics" and sometimes making brief appearances on stage.

When the curtain came down I took advantage of the club's excellent little bar to have my first meal of the day, washed down with a splendid beverage called "winter brew", which was a dark bitter beer. Then I caught the last underground train home to Wood Green, arriving there at about 12.30 am.

One day I detected an itch under my arm and when I scratched it I found that small particles of skin came away from what appeared to be a rash. Soon it spread down to my elbow, across my front and back to the centre of my body. Open blisters appeared, apparently caused by the inflammation of nerve ends. The pain was almost unendurable and kept me awake at nights sitting up in bed and rocking to and fro. This was in the days before effective pain-killers. It was diagnosed as shingles and the only remedy was the application externally of a cooling lotion, although my long-suffering wife did her best to mitigate my pain and discomfort. The doctor told me I was obviously overdoing it and my nerves were exploding in protest. It was essential I should reduce my activities and try to take things easier.

In the event change was imposed on me. One day the man who acted as part-time company secretary to the Mercantile Guardian called me into his office and told me about the wonderful new financial arrangement being set up to ensure that when employees became too old to work they had an income to supplement the very modest amount provided by the State. It was called a "company pension scheme". The company would contribute part of the necessary regular payments and the rest would be deducted from my salary. I laughed at him. I was in my mid 20s Retirement seemed a millennium away. He told me it was compulsory for all members of the staff to contribute. Unless I joined with the rest I would have to leave. It was anyway time to move on. I did so with regret as it had been a happy part of my life and it would also mean that I could no longer continue the arrangement with the New Lindsey.

In fact there was something prescient in my response. The company was negotiating a merger with a larger publishing house. The group that took the company over was in turn absorbed by an even larger one. The chairman of that international corporation famously plundered its pension scheme and ended his nefarious activities by committing suicide. What, I wonder, would have happened to my pension?

Chapter 18 - The lure of the lights

I became a feature writer on a glossy industrial magazine entitled Scope, where my work certainly provided me with a lot of it when it came to writing, but obviously did not allow me to spend half the day working at a theatre. I produced learned articles on such subjects as the Underground Gasification of Coal and the Industrial Use of Radio Isotopes, about neither of which had I the slightest knowledge. The former of these, of course, has a relevance nowadays, fifty years later, with the controversy over "fracking".

I was, however, still determined to continue my interest in the theatre. I particularly wanted to learn more about the developing art of theatrical lighting, but had been able to study it in only a rudimentary way at small theatres. I needed to get experience of it in the big houses of the West End. I knew someone who worked on the electrical staff of what was then known as the New Theatre in St Martin's Lane. He persuaded the Chief Engineer, Bill Bruce, to take me on as a regular member of the backstage staff, where I would be required to work only on performances in the evening and the occasional matinee.

This was a revolutionary time in theatrical lighting. Traditionally theatre stages and those acting on them had been lit by footlights, with similar rows of lights called battens hanging from the "flies", or lighting backcloths from below. The light was filtered through the three primary light colour system – red, green and blue, with an extra circuit for the blue because it let less light through. These could be varied in intensity according to the effect required. Used all together they produced a bright white light, which tended to be somewhat harsh and unnatural, in particular blotting out the actors' features. It was to mitigate this that actors used make-up, increasing the artificial effect.

Then everything began to change with innovations

originating, like many at this time, from the States. Producers like Elia Kazan wanted a greater intimacy for their scenes and, at the same time, a more realistic effect for the environment in which the plays were set. Most typical of this was the setting for Tennessee Williams' "A Streetcar Named Desire". The interior scenes for this were located in an island set surrounded by the streets of New Orleans. A flower-seller wandered across the fore stage offering "flowers for the dead". When Blanche covered the light because she could not bear a naked lamp, the lighting responded appropriately.

How was this achieved? Enter the "pattern 23", a small compact spotlight, hung from what was now called the spot-bar. New subtler colours were devised for the filters, offering modulated shades – straw, amber, pale pink, light blue. There was one that looked purple until it was lit, when it became a bright rose and for that reason was called surprise pink. It served to illuminate many a fairy queen in pantomime!

The systems for controlling the lights were also modified. Traditionally there were banks of dimmers, which could be linked together on a master board and worked by a wheel, producing various degrees of dimming and fades. These were replaced by buttons and electrical circuits and, of course, eventually by computers. Lighting a multiple set with these new techniques required a new set of skills, which the directors of the day did not always have. So a race of "lighting designers" emerged, foremost among whom in this country was Joe Davis, for whom I had the privilege of working.

The first play I was involved in at the New Theatre was the stage version of Gigi by Anita Loos. It had enjoyed considerable success on Broadway and the musical film had been a smash hit in this country. The star of the film, Leslie Caron, repeated her performance on the West End and the play was directed by her future husband Peter Hall. It was not, however, a success. Caron's French accent, so attractive in the film, was obviously an impediment when it came to projecting in the theatre. She became increasingly frustrated at her failure to communicate with the audience and I recall that she would storm off stage slamming the doors as she went. The backstage staff stood and waited for the final bang when she reached her dressing room.

I was fascinated by the scene changes. Trucks loaded with furniture and period properties were moved rapidly down or across stage and I can remember watching what was virtually half a room chasing a small plump stage-hand carrying a large aspidistra as he fled downstage. One of my jobs was to move the flood lights off stage that lit arches and doorways. On one occasion I almost crowned one of the principal actresses as I swung the lamp on its tall stand. She was Estelle Winwood, a *grande dame* on and off stage, who expressed her displeasure at my clumsiness in very unladylike language.

Gigi came off just before Christmas and the theatre went dark, so my services were not required. I feared I would be at a loose end theatrically, but the man who had introduced me to the New Theatre, Humphrey, had been appointed chief engineer at a very fine suburban theatre, the Hippodrome, Golders Green, which was known as the "number 1, number 1". When shows finished their run in the West End they would tour the country, playing the major theatres in provincial cities and towns. The grandest of these were known as the "number ones" and were often given majestic titles, such as the Theatre Royal", or "The Grand". On a lower level, hosting rather lesser fares, there were "Empires", many of them owned by the Moss Empire group. Below them again were the "Palaces", often specialising in weekly changes of "musical hall".

The Hippodrome epitomised everything that was glamorous about the theatre of that time, with its red velvet seats, gold fittings and a magnificent sweep of a grand circle. It would be presenting a traditional pantomime over the Christmas and Humphrey told me I would be working the lime-light. I wasn't quite sure what this involved, but the very word sounded exciting, epitomising as it did everything that was glamorous about the live theatre. After all Charlie Chaplin produced a film with that as its title.

It is so called because the light was originally achieved by burning a piece of lime to produce an intense white glow. Manipulating this steaming hot piece of equipment was obviously not a salubrious task and was only undertaken by youngsters struggling to gain their first foot on the theatrical ladder, or so poor they were unable to earn a living in any other way – not unlike me, in fact. The "lime-boy" was, therefore, known as the lowest form of animal life in the theatre, rather like the midshipman on the Bounty!

There were three of us, housed in a concrete bunker at the rear of the dress circle. It was sound-proof, airtight, hot and generally unpleasant. The lamp was a giant metal frame located close to one's cheek. The original lump of lime had been replaced by two carbon sticks, which we operators had to bring together so that they produced an even, bright light. Failure to do so accurately would reduce the flame to a splutter and the spot on the stage to a yellowy sausage.

There were levers to move from spot lenses to flood; and others to change the filter colours – surprise pink for the fairy queen, green for the demon king, amber for Abanaza, etc. On the opening night I was supposed to illuminate the fairy queen in a bright spot, but I pressed the flood switch by mistake, lighting the stage, the orchestra pit and the first few rows of the audience with surprise pink. The intercom, which was our only means of communication with back stage, burst into angry life with Humphrey threatening various kinds of painful death on me if I ever did that again. I did not!

It was a wonderful pantomime, worthy of the venue. The star was Laurie Lupino Lane, doyen of a great theatre family, whose father, Lupino Lane, was one of the most famous pantomime artistes in the first half of the 20th century. His career reached its apogee in the musical "For

Me and My Girl". Concerned to revive what he feared was a decline in the popularity of pantomime, Laurie had assembled a wonderful cast. His fellow comic was a well-known clown named George Truzzi. The wonderful Shani Wallis played Aladdin. A diminutive ingénue, Anthea Askey (daughter of the equally diminutive Arthur), was the Princess; and Dick Emery probably started his cross-dressing stage career as the Dame.

Many of Lupino Lane's famous sketches were revived in the show: the haunted castle, in which the principals were pursued through countless trap-doors by demons; the brokers' men who by breaking mountains of crockery should perhaps more rightly be called the breakers' men; the bucket-loads of rainbow coloured whitewash poured over various unfortunate members of the cast...

In our sound-proof concrete bunker we peered at the stage through a narrow slit in the wall and the only sound we received was through the intercom system. It had all the coldness and detachment of watching a television show, as we twiddled our controls and between cues talked, drank tea and ate our snacks. One day I received a summons to go backstage during the show. I went out through the metal door and the impact I received from that 2000-odd audience was palpable. It was like moving from the cold and damp of an English autumn into the sunshine and warmth of a Caribbean island. As I made my way round the back of the auditorium I was carried on a wave of human enjoyment reacting to the action on stage. This is what live theatre is all about, I thought. This what we are in danger of losing with our obsession with television.

The pantomime over I was fortunate enough to be invited back to the New Theatre to work on a rather special production. This was to be the stage version of Dylan Thomas's Under Milk Wood, which required a multiple set, built on several levels, representing the streets of llareggub (bugger-all backwards), and the rooms of its inhabitants. This obviously made full use of modern lighting techniques and I was delighted to find that Joe

Davis had been appointed lighting designer.

In addition to the main lighting on stage it was necessary to position a follow-spot from front of house to pick up the narrator. There was no limelight at the theatre, or secure housing for one, so it was decided that an area at the front of the gallery should be cordoned off to make way for a small spotlight. It did not have any special security arrangements and I wonder if this would be acceptable under modern health and safety rules.

I was given the job of working this spotlight, together with my own small electrical installation. I would join the audience in my roped-off section and, in effect, started the show. The two narrators had been combined into one and were spoken by Donald Houston, whose principal claim to fame up to that time was that he was the muscle-man who banged the gong to introduce the J. Arthur Rank films. He appeared on to a darkened stage and I had to shine a spot on to his face.

As will be imagined this was a heavy responsibility as I was working entirely on my own, without cues, surrounded by gallery theatre goers. If I failed to light him effectively the show would not start. I was still working on Scope at the time and it was not unknown for me to attend press receptions during the day. As many journalists will know these may be little more than "booze-ups". There were occasions when I arrived at the theatre somewhat the worse for wear, but it was still necessary for me to climb the stairs to the gallery and take my place under the curious gaze of the audience. Then I not only had to find Donald Houston's face with my little spot, but hold it steady until the rest of the stage lights came up! The Chief Engineer did look at me rather strangely once or twice when I arrived, but so far as I know was never aware how near the show was to disaster!

In addition to my work on the magazine I was writing a great deal, I produced an article describing my life at on the notorious Abadan run. Somewhat to my surprise it was published in what was then known as the Manchester

Guardian. I followed it up with articles on my amateur production of Antigone in the East End and on my exploits as a lime boy and this time they were accepted by The Times, which in those days, were, of course, published anonymously.

The actor playing Captain Cat in Under Milk Wood was William Squire, who was also a protégée of Philip Gibbons and had started his stage career in the Bethnal Green amateur drama group before my time there. He went to RADA and was a successful classical actor before eventually succumbing to the lure of a TV series. He saw my piece in the Guardian, which carried a by-line and asked if I had had any others published. I told him about The Times articles and this was greeted by him and others in the cast with great astonishment as I was probably the only lime-boy in the history of the theatre who was at the same time contributing to The Times!

Under Milk Wood was only moderately successful on stage. It was written specifically for performance on radio and is not really a play as such. I think I can claim, however, to have been the only one to sit through every performance and a few years later I put the experience to good use when I appeared in a production at what was called a "Residence Centre Theatre" run by the Arts Council in West London. A group calling itself Cygnet Productions had been producing plays there and decided to present Under Milk Wood. I was cast as Willie Nillie Postman and a Drowned Man.

I do not think the director took kindly to me. He complained that as a Drowned Man I could not be heard and when I used a full voice accused me of shouting. He pretty well left me alone as Willie Nillie, however, and my encounter with Mrs Ogmore-Pritchard was a joy. She was played by a wonderful character actress named Dorothea Phillips, who, as she would readily acknowledge, was not the most attractive of women, saying that her face was what kept her in television work. She suggested that we could easily knock off our little scene together, which we did.

About now I encountered a paradox ("a paradox, a paradox, a most amusing paradox"). I was a journalist and longed to work full time in the professional theatre. Occupying a desk facing me in the Scope office was a young man whose name was O'Connor. One day I told him about my interest in the theatre and how I dreamed of becoming an actor. He expressed his astonishment, explaining that he came from a theatrical background and his only ambition was to be a journalist. He had been under constant pressure to work in show-business, but he hated the whole idea. His father was a singer, an uncertain occupation financially and emotionally that had caused him and his mother much unhappiness. His name struck a chord with me and I asked him what his father's name was. He told me it was Cavan.

Cavan O'Connor was famous. Better known as the Wandering Vagabond, he was frequently on radio and topped the bill at music halls throughout the country. So here was his son, a young man with the opportunity to make his way in show business, but who hated it and wanted only to be a journalist. He had set his foot firmly on that ladder and was determined to achieve his ambition. He put me to shame! What was I doing, languishing in editorial work when I had opportunities – and possibly the talent – to make something of myself in the theatre? From that moment I determined to follow my star, to whichever side of the limelight it led me.

Chapter 19 – Are you one of us?

To progress in the theatre, however, I would have to find work in the provinces and that would mean leaving my wonderful London. It was the advertisement in The Stage for a stage director and occasional actor at Northampton Rep. that eventually decided my fate. Housed in the splendid Theatre Royal this had the reputation of being the best "weekly" repertory company in the country, placing it, as it were, at the top of the third division (the second comprised those provincial theatres producing plays every fortnight, while the first, or premier, division was occupied by companies enjoying the luxury of three-weekly runs, or longer).

Without any great expectation of success I attended an interview with the director. He did not mention acting directly, but I knew from experience that working back stage would lead to opportunities to don the grease paint. He questioned me about my stage experience, seemed surprised that I had spent so much of my life working as a journalist, looked at me very keenly and said: "It is important that you should be one of us. Are you?" I assumed he was anxious to be convinced I was serious in my ambition to join a professional theatre company, I assured him that I was.

Looking back now I wonder how I could have been so naïve. But why should I think he meant anything else? I liked to regard myself as a professional and I was applying for a job, not a sexual proclivity. Throughout my life I have tended to accept people for what they are. What they do in bed does not concern me and seems irrelevant – until, that is, they try to get me there with them. Even the experience of being fumbled in the austere environment of a London office or chased around the cabins of an ocean going liner did not alert me to the nature of the company I was joining. It was some months later and I would be settled in the job before I realised what he meant!

Anyway, to my surprise he offered me the job. It was to be a new life, working for the first time in a fully professional environment. It would mean lodging locally and I was reluctant to leave my long-suffering wife, although not entirely sorry to turn my back on a house that still held so many emotionally destructive memories. Fortunately, in caring for my children Doris was assisted by my mother, who although now in her 80s, was still very lively and could frequently be seen running for a bus in order to play the piano "for the old folk" at a local pensioners' club!

I had no difficulty finding "digs" in Northampton. In those days there were always plenty of these in provincial theatre towns and the landladies of many have become the stuff of legend. The theatre itself was a thing of beauty. It was then in its 75th year, which the company celebrated on 5th May 1959 with a production of Twelfth Night, the play with which it opened in 1884. On that occasion Malvolio was played by a celebrated actor of the day, Edward Compton, and to introduce this new production his daughter, Fay Compton, also a famous actress, gave a celebratory oration.

What must be amazing to modern observers is that this theatre, holding a few hundred seats, was able to maintain its existence entirely on the proceeds of eight performances a week, supporting a company comprising: director, designer, back stage staff of six, as well as front of house manager and assistant and all those who worked in the box office and as ushers. All this in addition to the regular cast of actors, of which there were at least eight, sometimes augmented by guest artistes.

What is even more astonishing is that throughout the country in towns and cities, large and small, there were theatres offering similar fare, employing professional actors and stage staff and all part of the national industry known as "the theatre". Everyone was dedicated to the work. Opportunities for socialising were rare and there was no attempt to establish what in modern times would have been regarded as team-building. The business of putting on a different play every week was very demanding and to give the cast their due they were concerned to ensure that their presentations were as professional as could be achieved within the limitations of their exhausting schedule. The number of hours people worked were not relevant. Employment laws did not apply. When actors were not performing they were rehearsing, and when they were not doing either, they were learning lines for the next play and even reading or preparing a script for the one after that.

There was a tendency among those in the more exalted levels of the professional theatre, such as those working regularly in London's West End, to regard weekly rep theatres with a certain condescension, even contempt. Yet the best of them - and Northampton certainly was one of the best – managed an extraordinarily high degree of professionalism both in the standard of the acting and in the quality of the staging. They certainly managed to bring in a loyal audience that filled the house week after week.

When one considers the exigencies under which they worked one can only look back in wonder at what they managed to achieve. The working week started on Tuesday morning, when the cast assembled for the first rehearsal of next production. Most of them would have endured an opening night of another play on the Monday. They would have received their scripts a few days in advance (those with leading parts sometimes earlier) and would have had time to read through and mark-up the scenes and dialogue relating to them.

The theatre's scenic artist would have produced a ground plan for the set, which would have been marked out either on stage, or in a rehearsal room. Positions of doors, windows, etc, were indicated and rehearsal furniture placed into position. Acting editions of the plays usually contained the lay-out of the West End run, which had to be modified, sometimes drastically, to fit the stage's smaller dimensions. Rehearsal time was obviously limited so the original moves were usually retained as far as possible, although when I later came to direct plays I would try to revise as many as possible in order to make them work more effectively in the smaller environment

The first rehearsal was for what was known as blocking, when the whole business of the action, including any changes in dialogue, would be confirmed and marked by the actors in their scripts, and by one of the stage management staff who would be acting as prompter for the show. The prompt script would also be marked up for lighting and sound cues, which would later be listed and passed on to the electrician and technical stage manager. All the furniture, properties, and technical requirements for the show were listed in a hard-cover property book, foolscap sized and ruled in appropriate columns.

Hopefully the blocking would be finished by lunchtime, usually one o'clock. This would leave time for the cast to rest in readiness for the evening performance and begin to learn their lines. Those for act 1 were expected to be learnt for the Wednesday morning's rehearsal. There would be no rehearsal on the Thursday because of the afternoon matinee, so that lines for both acts 2 and 3 had to be learnt by Friday. The cast was expected to be "word-perfect" by Saturday, which was a very busy day. In the morning there would be a "run-through" of the whole play, with sound effects and all rehearsal props. Once again it would be hoped to finish by a reasonably early lunch as there would be a matinee of the current production at 5.30, with the final performance at 8.15.

When the curtain came down on the Saturday night the technical stage staff would dismantle the set and put the scenery up for the next week's show on stage ready for the set-up on Monday. If it was an elaborate set they might have to continue on the next day. It was rare for the cast to rehearse on Sunday, although those with larger parts might get together to work on them privately. Otherwise, they spent the day polishing their lines, doing their laundry and preparing their costumes for the forthcoming show. Some of them even found time to take a little rest! The dress rehearsal took place during the day on Monday. If there were problems it might go on all day, even being known to continue behind a lowered "iron curtain" with the audience arriving!

The sets comprised the canvas flats traditionally used on stage for decades. In former years the scenery had been changed in full view of the audience, being pushed on to the stage along grooves or slots in the floor. Then there was the famous occasion when the front curtain was lowered and only a few seconds later raised again revealing to a delighted and astonished audience a complete change of scenery. After that it became the norm and a tradition emerged that however elaborate the setting the curtain should never remain down for longer than 45 seconds. The flats were ten to 20 feet high and were run into position (usually single-handedly) by stage-hands. A line was attached to the top of one flat, taken round a cleat at the bottom and "thrown" with a twist of the wrist to a cleat at the top of another. Skilled stage hands could do this in the dark! Flats were of different widths to provide variation and opportunities for alcoves, with gaps for door and windows, the frames of which were inserted after they were positioned.

Northampton's high standard of presentation among repertory theatres was partly due to its resident designer, Osborne Robinson, who liked to be known as a "stage artist". He had established something of a reputation in the world of theatre design and had written a standard work on the subject. He was a large, bearded man, who could become quite emotional and breathe heavily over the frustrations that the limitations of a repertory theatre placed upon his creativity. He was very much of a traditionalist and did not approve of the new techniques that were being introduced, such as the introduction of moulding and texture. He believed that the architectural features of an interior could be represented by painting them on the canvas flats. I sometimes wonder how he reacted to the introduction of multiple sets and movable trucks.

So I was joining a well-established professional company with a good reputation. My role meant I had control over all aspects of production, answerable only to the director. At the start I encountered a certain hostility from some members of the company, which I put down to the fact that the person I replaced had been very popular and I was continually being compared unfavourably with him. Also it did not help that, like the traditional new broom, I attempted to instil greater discipline in backstage behaviour and time-keeping, where the popularity of my predecessor had led to a more relaxed regime. Fortunately, although some members of the cast resented this, I had the support of the director and, indeed, of the theatre management generally.

As the season progressed, however, I began to realise that the antagonism towards me owed its origins to something rather more personal. It became apparent that I had misinterpreted the director's question and obviously was not "one of them". These were the days when a person's sexual proclivities, if they deviated from the norm, were closely hidden. The situation was aggravated when my wife came to visit me. She was a pretty young mother, and had a light-hearted and outwardly happy disposition, the very antithesis of some cast members, who went about their business and their relationships with a kind of dark broodiness. They did not make her welcome and I did not inflict the experience on her again.

My popularity was not improved by the fact that the director obviously found I was a useful addition to the cast of character actors. Obviously I took full advantage of this and some of the cast were jealous because they thought I deprived them of opportunities to play certain parts. Older, more experienced, members of the company, however, began to accept the situation and respect my ability to hold my own on stage and contribute effectively to scenes.

Our production of Twelfth Night, for example,

obviously made considerable demands on a relatively small company and I was given the insignificant part of "An Officer". I would not have expected this to cause any resentment, but I found that the young actor playing Valentine complained bitterly that I had more lines than he.

There was another piece of casting that created particular envy. I cannot remember the name of the play, but it took place in the bar of a public house. The principal character was a harridan of a woman who dominated the action and the dialogue. I played her hen-pecked husband, sitting by her, obeying her every wish, enduring her nagging, but never saying a word for the entire evening. Towards the end of the play, I was required to break my silence by lurching to my feet and bursting drunkenly into song at the top of my voice: "It's the same the whole world over. It's the poor what gets the blame. It's the rich what gets the gravy. Isn't it a blooming shame!" Then I staggered off to the gents accompanied by thunderous applause.

Apart from the acting I derived a great deal of satisfaction from my work as stage director. Running such a tight schedule obviously depended upon back-stage efficiency and effective coordination between the artistic and technical departments. As a stage director for me the high spot was our production of the famous old classic "The Ghost Train" - the only success of its author, Arnold Ridley, who later turned up triumphantly on television in Dad's Army.

It was possible to produce it using a recorded sound track, but this lacked verisimilitude and the director was anxious to apply the original sound effects, which were set out in the acting edition. This involved a backstage staff of about 12, which I had literally to conduct from the prompt corner. The play takes place in a station waiting room and the sound effects of various trains have to be simulated. The first is of a train arriving, produced by percussionists, one on kettle drum, another on bass. Finally, a heavy garden roller is rolled across slats behind the scene to provide vibrations so realistic they are felt by the audience. The train stops, then departs with all the necessary door opening and closing, whistles, guard commands, etc. At one time an express passes through at speed. Then there is the ghost train itself, which involves a window of the room being smashed.

Another immensely and difficult play from a stage management point of view was The Diary of Anne Frank, which had been adapted for the stage with skill and sensitivity. The whole life of that tragic family over their years in the cellar had to be reproduced. It began with the post-war discovery of the diary, reverted back to the family's first arrival in its new home, then each scene showed them at different times progressively throughout their stay, until the Nazi forces are heard breaking down the outside door and the play reverts to the present time. Every item used by the family during their stay had to be provided as properties, removed and changed with the passage of time, together with the movement of furniture, all in black-outs, as obviously the curtain could not be lowered so frequently. To link the scenes music was played and Anne's voice was heard reading her diary, involving carefully orchestrated sound cues both live and recorded.

In addition to the difficulties backstage it made considerable demands on the cast in terms of interpretation and acting skill so that it was one of the rare occasions when two weeks were provided for rehearsal. The unremitting and tragic nature of the story itself also had a tremendous emotional impact on all of us and when the curtain came down after the first performance I am sure I was not the only one to find myself silently weeping.

Perhaps this kind of shared experience between cast and stage management helped to lessen any hostility towards me and towards the end of my time there the atmosphere began to change. It was helped when a couple of new actors were appointed who obviously did not share the prejudices of current company members. Their influence led to rather more socialising, and I remember particularly the celebration of someone's birthday with a party that went on all night. I strolled back to my digs in the early morning mist alongside the beautiful river that runs through the town, feeling much more content with my lot.

One of the newcomers was a handsome leading man who turned out to be your average heavy drinking, womanising male. Soon after he arrived he noticed that I carried a bottle opener on my key-ring and said he knew we would get along fine. And we did although I was not, and never have been, a heavy drinker. He was Nicholas Courtney, who achieved television fame some years later as a military officer in Dr Who.

Chapter 20 – The show must go on – or must it?

My stay at Northampton was rewarding and towards the end even enjoyable. But obviously I could not stay there forever. The drive is constantly upwards, like the mountaineer who cannot stop until he has reached the summit. My ultimate goal was the West End of London, but I could not leap directly there from a humble provincial rep., however well reputed. Then I found a halfway house that I thought might help me on the way.

I became stage director of the Meadow Players, resident company at the Oxford Playhouse. This was the chance of a life-time as the theatre was one of the most prestigious repertory venues in the country. It had started in the 1950s as a fortnightly rep. with a high cultural standard in its choice of plays. Its season in the autumn of 1956, for example, included Giraudoux's Electra, The Knights of the Round Table by Jean Cocteau, and a new play by Peter Ustinov called The Empty Chair - the sort of fare not attempted by your average rep. By the time I joined the company, in 1960, its performances were lasting a month and the standard of production meant it had become an important try-out theatre for productions on their way to the West End. One of the most significant of these was the first stage adaptation of the novel A Passage to India.

The company's director, Frank Hauser had a talent not only for selecting interesting plays, but also persuading actors of quality, sometimes former stars, who might have been languishing out of the lime-light for a while, to return to the stage, with supporting casts of first class players. My first production at the theatre, Bernard Shaw's The Apple Cart, was a typical example. Sebastian Shaw, who had at one time been much better known both on the stage and in films, played the lead. Others in the cast included Harold Lang, Alan Edwards, Heather Chasen, Noel Dyson and Adrienne Corri. Needless to say, I was delighted to be among such company.

The next production was Naked, by the Italian playwright Luigi Pirandello, who was having something of a vogue at the time as the writer of Six Characters in Search of an Author. It was to be directed by the theatre's co-director, Minos Volanaikis. A very well-known film and stage actress was to play the lead and among the supporting cast were several fine actors who would later became well known on television, including David Jackson and Frank Thornton.

The star's partner, a young man beginning to make a name for himself in films, played the small part of Consul Grotti. Those of us who watched from the side decided he was not a very good actor, perhaps because he was miscast. He appeared out of place on stage and didn't seem to know what to do with his hands. He was, however, tall and very good looking, and certainly had a kind of presence on stage. We thought if he had a future at all it would be in films. That assessment was prescient. The actress was Diane Cilento and the actor was, of course, Sean Connery.

In his desire to maintain an acceptable cultural level and to encourage new talent, Frank Hauser was not one to baulk at taking chances. One day he gave me the script of a new play to read and asked for my opinion. I read it and thought it a rather pedestrian piece. The principal character was apparently based on an acquaintance of the author. This man had led a somewhat licentious life with little regard for his wife and family and others he encountered. I was surprised at the author's unrestrained depiction of a man he seemed to regard as something of a hero and expressed my concern to Hauser at the possibility of a libel action. He dismissed it, explaining that the man had read the script and was delighted to see himself depicted in what to him was a favourable light. The production went ahead with Victor Maddern, an actor who later made quite a name for himself in both film and television, playing the lead.

The play ran for three weeks and on the final Friday morning Hauser summoned me urgently to his office in London, where I found him and Minos in deep discussion. It appeared that the play had been called off and could not be shown again as a libel action had been threatened. I could not refrain from reminding him of my warning and asked why the man involved had changed his mind. Hauser said he had not. He had been delighted by the play, but when his wife saw it for the first time she was so horrified at the way she was portrayed that she stormed into the management office and demanded that it be taken off forthwith. That was on the previous night.

On the following Monday the play was booked to open at the Cambridge Arts Theatre, for a two-week run. There would be heavy financial penalties for cancelling the booking. What could be done? Frank told me he and Minos had decided on a solution. A few weeks previously the company's production of A Woman of No Importance, starring Michael Dennison and Dulcie Gray, which had transferred from Oxford to the West End, ended its successful run. He proposed to revive it in Cambridge.

I received the proposal with astonishment. It had been a major West End production. The cast had been paid off, the scenery put into store in south London, furniture dispersed to the various antique and other dealers who had supplied it, costumes and wigs returned to the hirers. Transport had been arranged to carry one load from Oxford to Cambridge on the Saturday night, but not to collect various items from addresses in London on the following Monday. There was a weekend and one day in which to present a complex production at what was to me a strange theatre.

Michael Dennison was a major star and a theatre producer in his own right and had a reputation as a stickler for precision regarding anything that might affect his performance or that of his equally well-known wife,. The stage management had to be meticulous. I drew Hauser's attention to the problems I had to face, but he said he had full confidence in the ability of myself and my staff to overcome them. It was a confidence I did not share.

There is a tradition in the professional theatre, that, come what may, the curtain must go up. On the opening night in Cambridge it was achieved. The artists had their costumes and wigs, the scenery was in position, the lighting had been set. My stage manager called "half-hour please" over the intercom as usual at 35 minutes before curtain up. As a courtesy to the star I knocked on Michael Dennison's door and invited him to view the stage. He said he was sure that Dulcie would also like to see it so the two of them came down and walked the set, examining the scenery and the furniture and particularly the hand props. My heart had been in my mouth so I was relieved that they seemed to approve of everything. As they left the stage Michael stopped by a desk he used on several occasions in the play, picked up a pen and showed it to me. It was important, he said, to place it correctly with the handle towards the right, not the left!

It had been a testing time, but the next production with the Meadow Players proved perhaps even more demanding. In order to give the resident company a well-earned rest at Christmas, a visiting company had always been invited to take over the theatre for the traditionally seasonal show. This year Hauser decided the Meadows Players should present its own production and the choice was Brandon Thomas's classic "Charley's Aunt". I was quite happy be involved in what is regarded as the best farce ever written, but I was not prepared for the work and stress involved.

The central comic role of Lord Fancourt Babberley was to be played by Bob Grant, who became well-known in later years on television, principally for his role in On the Buses. The rest of the cast, as usual, was made up of highly professional actors, many of whom would also later appear in various television roles, such as Anthony Valentine, Christopher Guinee, and John Nettleton.

Although the company did not have a break, it appeared this did not apply to Frank Hauser as he appointed a guest director. This man shall be nameless, but in my opinion he walked through the production in a pedestrian manner and did little to assist the cast or bring out the play's considerable comic value.

Christmas shows are usually expected to be something of a romp and on the surface it might appear that this light-hearted comedy would not make particular demands on resources, but it certainly did, particularly in a theatre with the reputation of the Playhouse where only the strictest attention to historical detail was acceptable. It is, of course, a costume play, and even acquiring the necessary props of the period made heavy demands. It is in three acts, each requiring a strong, well-built set, able to withstand the various antics the Aunt and other characters indulged in, such as climbing through windows, swinging on door frames, etc.

After the rehearsal on the Saturday before Christmas we cleared the stage and started to set up that night. From then until the curtain came down after the first performance on Tuesday night, I did not sleep, except for an occasional cat-nap on an armchair backstage; and my only food comprised the pies and fish and chips brought in to me. We barely managed to get everything ready in time for a belated dress rehearsal that had to be continued behind the iron curtain while the audience was arriving

The play was received by delighted audiences and once it was settled in I was allowed to take a break. I returned to London, where I fell ill and went to bed with severe influenza. It was the last I saw of Oxford. I had worked myself to the point of collapse. I had been involved in a number of interesting, rewarding productions, but had no opportunity to get on the stage and act. This was 1960. I was 33 years of age. In ten years I had seen more of the professional theatre than some people manage to achieve in a lifetime, but it was still not enough. I was back in London and there I hoped to stay.

Chapter 21 – Resting

The life of an actor and his approach to the work must resemble in some respects that of the tight-rope walker. He (or she) lives only for the moments up on the wire, balancing between triumph and disaster. The problem is what to do with the time on the ground. In the acting profession it is called resting – a misnomer if there ever was one because he (or she) usually works harder then in order to pay the bills and settle the debts he acquired when working.

I left the relative security of Northampton and Oxford and set my feet on uncertain ground again. My first priority was to earn money. As a self-employed actor I could not draw on the benefit of what was known as the "dole". I had to find myself temporary employment. Fortunately, although I had always regretted not receiving a more academic education, the "commercial" training I received at Tottenham Technical College was a life-saver. I had been taught to touch-type at speed.

I discovered there were companies known as law stationers. They acted, in effect, as lawyers' clerks, producing under contract and to order such documents as formal agreements, contracts, wills, leases and their counterparts. One such was Stephen Cox and Company, a small family business located in Holborn and run by two brothers – Raymond and Jack Cox. I do not know if Stephen existed, but if he did he was not in evidence.

The two brothers were very different in personality. Raymond was quiet and reticent, concerning himself mainly with the administration of the firm. Jack was a fiery, pragmatic character responsible for day-to-day operation and in particular for ensuring that his motley crew performed to the very exacting standards required by the clients. He employed a regular staff of typists, mainly female, but to cope with the uneven work demand he called on a small army of part-time workers in a variety of jobs: reading and checking documents, binding them, sewing with green tape, collecting and delivering the work. He welcomed my occasional contributions between theatrical engagements because not only could I type rapidly and accurately, but could read at top speed.

Accuracy was paramount. In those days, of course, there were no computers. Legal documents of all kinds were produced on vast typewriters, with especially long carriages to cope with the parchment-style documents. The "engrossments" of leases and other forms of agreement were produced by one operator and their "counterparts" by another. The lease was then read out loud by one person at top speed while another followed the counterpart. The theory was that two operators using different machines would not make the same mistake. It seemed to work! Typists, working at speeds of up to 60 words a minute, were allowed to erase and replace errors except wills where it was illegal.

Speed was also of the essence, as the documents were often required at short notice to conclude a contractual arrangement or perhaps as evidence in court proceedings. Not only were the fingers expected to move with extreme rapidity on the heavy equipment, but reading was also conducted at a rate that made it scarcely audible. Jack was particularly skilled at this. When a member of staff arrived in the office, without giving him or her time to remove a coat or hat, he would thrust a counterpart document into their hand and rattle off at top speed.

One day I was working on my own in an office on a lower floor. A rather scruffy individual appeared, thrust a document into my hand for copying and left. It turned out to be a badly written near-pornographic description of the sexual activities between two people. Suspecting a practical joke, I telephoned Jack to ask him what it was all about. He responded with fury telling me that it was court evidence needed urgently and why was I wasting time questioning it?

One day I found myself engrossing the contract for

Sean Connery to play the part of James Bond. Our work was, of course, subject to the strictest confidentiality, but after all these years I do not think he would mind if I recall that not only was his salary astronomical, but the agreement stipulated he should enjoy first class travel facilities, the finest hotels and a number of suits tailored every year in Saville Row. The previous time I had encountered this talented actor he played a small part in a production for which I had a degree of responsibility. Now I was glad of the few pennies earned from the privilege of typing his contract. Such is theatrical life!

A great advantage of the work was that some of it could be carried on at home, where I had a typewriter. In the office one was paid by the hour; at home one received so much per 72 words (yes 72), with extra when including carbon copies. It was gruelling work and I was quite glad when a more fascinating – and rewarding – resting job came my way.

The Government had legalised gambling and the first casinos were being opened in London. There was no stock-pile of experienced staff to work on the tables and the largest and most luxurious of these in central London was offering what seemed a quite princely wage for potential croupiers and dealers to train. Once employed the remuneration they earned was even more attractive particularly as at that time it was supplemented by tips.

An additional advantage for someone like me was that the hours were from eight in the evening until four in the morning, leaving the day clear to look for theatre work. Also at the time I was planning my own theatre production company and, in addition to attending auditions I was beginning to hold them myself, interview potential cast, read plays and even, eventually, rehearse productions.

I took the course and in due time found myself in a vast red plush and gilt room, hung with chandeliers, adjacent to one of London's most luxurious hotels. Dressed in a dinner suit and black tie I stood and awaited my customers with some trepidation behind a blackjack table, of which there were half a dozen forming an arc in what was known as a pit. An "inspector" sat at each table watching every move made by the dealer and the punters. Strolling from table to table keeping a close eye on dealers, players and inspectors was a "pit boss". In the centre of the room were several roulette tables in both forms: the polite and dignified French, and the faster, hands-on, louder American version. As most people know, French roulette involves the use of the *croup* to gather in the smart polished chips, hence the word croupier. In American roulette the croupier sweeps in plastic pieces with his arms and hands.

Beyond the roulette tables were the "crap" games, a noisy activity in which players threw the dice across tables and shouted numbers at them as if they could influence the way in which they landed. There would then be expostulations of triumph or despair depending on the results. At the far end of the room was the more dignified environment of the baccarat table, an arcane mystery for which very special skills were required in its dealers. It was presided over at that time, if my memory serves me correctly, by the captain of the British bridge team.

It was a bit like being on a film set. The principal actors were at the tables, either playing or dealing. The extras wandered about in their smart clothes, some of them in evening dress, viewing the action and presumably muttering "rhubarb, rhubarb". Presiding over all this activity was the floor manager accompanied by one or more minions. The Saville-Row-suited general manager of the casino was seldom seen, and when he occasionally did condescend to make his appearance all those whose job it was to ensure smooth running of the operation would be seized with tension as if they were being visited by royalty.

Early in my experience, and still somewhat of a novice, I remember standing alone at the table without any punters, three packs of cards unused in their shoe, a tray of £1 and £5 chips before me. A gentleman dressed in the robes of an Arabic potentate left the baccarat table and came across to my table, on which he placed a square plaque that I realised was valued at £10,000. Then he sat and waited expectantly for me to deal the cards. The inspector saw the look of panic in my eyes and hastily summoned the pit boss, who ordered the tray of chips to be replaced by one containing only those with a value of £25. Then, much to my relief, he took over as dealer and I watched as the visitor steadily relinquished the money he had won.

In time I developed a facility in the work: shuffling the packs of cards; drawing them from their "shoe" and distributing them correctly and neatly in front of the patrons; pointing to their hands and calculating their value; withdrawing those that were "busted", pulling the chips out of the tray and presenting them in little piles against the stake when the patrons won; collecting them when they lost; gathering up the cards with a little flourish. I became very adept at handling the chips, twiddling them in my fingers, demonstrating little tricks, which were frowned upon by one's superiors: "We were not there to play games", they said. One I was particularly proud of comprised holding three chips between thumb and third finger, then with the other fingers of the same hand, removing the centre chip, turning it and replacing it between the other two.

At regular intervals we were relieved from our posts and allowed to take a break in a rest room. I spent the time reading the scripts of plays for the company I was proposing to set up. We would be called back on to the floor by one of the assistant floor managers and one night a tall, blonde young man came in to do so. His mood was arrogant towards what he obviously regarded as a lower order of humanity. As he passed me sitting with my legs stretched out reading a play by Noel Coward, he kicked my feet and told me to get moving.

I put my book away and went out into the casino. He was in the centre of the crowded room surrounded by the great and good of London high society. I walked across to him and put my face quite close to his. "Don't ever kick me again", I said, "or you will regret it for the rest of your life". I have no idea to this day what made me do it and where I got the courage. It was like a scene from a Hollywood movie. The young man went the colour of his starched shirt. He looked from side to side as if wondering whether to summon security support. Then he mumbled a kind of apology. I nodded as if to say: OK, but don't do it again, and went to my table. From then on he treated me with more respect.

The security restraint on us lowly croupiers was immensely tight, resembling the kind of surveillance that might be encountered by the inmates of a top-security prison. Once inside the building we were not allowed out until our tour of duty ended. It was forbidden to make phone calls out (this was, of course, in the days before mobile phones), presumably in case we revealed to some potential gambler outside that there was a run on the bank! Before we left the table after a stint of dealing we were required to "clean" our hands, which involved passing the palms together and holding them up presumably to show we were not purloining chips, although exactly what we were supposed to do with them I do not know.

The money received from punters was pushed down a slot in the table by a plastic spatula. Tips went into a separate slot, to be added to a tronc, from which we each received a share with our salaries according to our status. At the end of the night's gaming the money boxes were removed and the takings counted under the watchful eyes of one or more overseers.

Among all this security there is, however, a beautiful irony. When I left the casino's employ I was given my PAYE form, showing the amount of salary I had received and the tax deducted from it. It also showed my share of the tips, but, although tax had been deducted from this at source, the amount was not recorded on the form. In case this would create problems when I made my annual return to Customs and Excise, I telephoned the casino's head office and queried it, only to be told that this element of my pay was not handled there. It was, they said, the responsibility of the casino itself.

I was becoming deeply involved in my new production company at the time and let the matter rest. Years later, however, I read in the national press that the manager of that casino was tried *in abstentio* for fraud, some of which related to retention of tax deducted from staff. It appears he was involved in other criminal activities and the judge at the trial described him, who at that time was languishing in Singapore, as the wickedest man he had ever encountered! As Juvenal said : *quis custodiet ipsos custodes.*

When my own theatre production company did not prosper I found it necessary to take up casino work again. This time it was in one smaller and less grand. It was one of two opened by the well-known comedian Charlie Chester, opposite each other in a Soho back street, conveniently nestling beside the stage doors of Shaftesbury Avenue theatres. One was called the Golden Nugget and I obtained employment at the other, which was named after the owner.

The clientele comprised generally small-time gamblers and the atmosphere was much more relaxed. Nevertheless many of those playing there had a very real addiction and if I had been a gambler myself my experience there would have turned me against it for life. The trouble was, it seemed to me, that the punters were not engaged in a "gamble" as such. There was a statistical certainty that they would lose. Except when playing poker against other gamblers, the odds were stacked against them.

It appears that initially when the government of the day decided to legalise casino gambling it was proposed that the odds should be set so that they did not favour the casino owners, the moral principle being that no one should profit from another's losses. Those who were intending to open the venues pointed out that if the odds were even they would in effect not have an income. The government suggested they could achieve this by charging for entry, to which the casino owners pointed out that customers could hardly be expected to pay an entrance fee in order to lose their money. Eventually, agreement was reached allowing for a five per cent margin in favour of the management. In roulette this was represented by the zeros added to the numbers on a roulette table, leaving the odds for winning only 36 to 1 against 37 numbers. Odds for the other games were arranged accordingly, meaning in effect that over the longer-term, statistically the punter could not win.

It is said that gambling is in many ways a more destructive form of addiction than drugs or alcohol, if only because there is no medical cure. It has no physical impact on the body, but it can have a destructive psychological impact on the sufferer and, collaterally, those close to him or her. This was certainly demonstrated to me during my time at Charlie Chester's. On one occasion a young man had won about £20,000 on roulette, which seemed a lot for a small casino to lose in one night and I commiserated with the manager. He shrugged his shoulders and pointed out that people who won that sort of money were usually regular gamblers and he would, therefore, soon play it all back and more besides.

Soon after starting at Charlie Chester's I noticed an elderly man dressed in what appeared to be a rather well-worn sports jacket. Closer examination revealed that it was, in fact, cashmere and the man obviously had at one time been well-to-do. I asked a fellow dealer about him and was told his name was Cecil. He had been an inventor had a fortune from one of his inventions and was continuing to receive lucrative royalties. He was, however, an addictive gambler and to try and preserve some of his wealth his relatives had acquired a power of attorney and placed his funds in secure accounts, from which he received only a monthly stipend. When that ran out he was driven to hang about successful gamblers in the hope that they would stake him a pound or two so that he could continue playing.

The real destructive force of gambling came home to me one night when a young man was playing blackjack at my table into the early hours of the morning. He had lost all his money and was fiddling with his last remaining chip. Both I and my inspector urged him to go home. He said he could not. He did not have the courage. He had left home that day with the money in his pocket to pay for his family's holiday and he had just lost it all. His wife would be waiting for him.

Chapter 22 – Auditions, schools and the Method

Torture is relatively unknown in Great Britain today, but there is one area where the mental form at least still survives. It is known as the audition. Surprisingly it has been introduced as a feature of everyday life on television, with those participating finding themselves trapped in situations they were unprepared for and have been unable to escape. Viewers are invited to watch, much as audiences crowded to see the pillory, the stocks, drawing/hanging/quartering, in mediaeval times.

Auditions were – and probably still are - an important element in the lives of anyone with aspirations to participate in what is now sometimes called the entertainment business. The main purpose of attending was because they offered the possibility – however remote – of employment. I also saw them as opportunities to practise my acting technique and singing ability and they helped in the important business of overcoming nerves, removing the dread potential of one day suffering from stage fright, the premise being if you could survive the exigencies of a audition you could endure anything..

Having to audition for speaking parts held little terrors for me and I always presented myself as an actor who could sing. Even my reading experience with Stephen Cox proved useful when asked to read from a strange text. My own set pieces included Faustus's dying speech, Shakespeare's Seven Ages of Man speech from As You Like It and Andrey's speech from Tchekov's The Three Sisters.

I was always more nervous when I was expected to sing. I felt reasonably secure with songs I had learnt and practised, but uncertain if I was asked to sing something new, as I could not sight-read music. The reverse seemed to be the case for those who were primarily singers when they were required to speak dialogue, but I always envied them their natural voices and their ability to sing from a score they had not prepared in advance.

There were basically two kinds of audition: the "open" and those involving an appointment with a management, which would take place at a specified time, in an office, rehearsal room, or perhaps on the stage of a theatre. One cold February morning I was sent by an agent to audition for work at the famous Regent's Park Open Air Theatre, which I had visited as a member of the audience on a number of occasions. The director at that time was the great character actor Robert Atkins, who had a reputation as a fearsome actor/manager. His performance as Bottom was acknowledged as the greatest ever. I was also totally in awe at his skill and artistry as Caliban in The Tempest, when his rendering of the "isle is full of noises" speech left me and probably many others of his audience in tears.

When I arrived at the Park I found I was not alone. The great man glared at the shivering group who had dared to defile his precious turf. It was like the captain of the England cricket team having to interview a group of apprentice players on the pitch at Lords. We gave him our names and he noted that one, in particular, had been sent by a particular agent. That aspirant was singled out and asked to stand on one side.

Then he turned his beady eye on me, to whom he seemed to take an instant dislike. He told me to audition first and settled himself on a seat about half-way up the green sward of the "auditorium". I had prepared the dying speech of Faustus from the Marlowe play and began; "Now Faustus thou hast but one bare hour to live – " He did not seem to be paying much attention so I tried using more voice. He fiddled in his waistcoat pocket. I spoke even louder, but still without making any impression. I remembered all my voice production lessons and took particular care over my diction, but he continued to search in his pockets. It appeared he was having a great deal of trouble plugging in his hearing aid.

Eventually he dismissed my valedictory efforts with a

wave of a majestic hand and asked if I had anything funny prepared. I suggested All The World's A Stage. "I don't think that's very funny", the great man said and only allowed me to reach the third age before he dismissed me with ill-concealed contempt. I was not invited back.

As a post script to this a few years later I was rehearsing in a crypt under the church of St Martins in the Field and on one occasion had to leave the rehearsal room. In the corridor I encountered Atkins, who was berating one of the members of his company. Their voices – particularly his – were loud and unrestrained and I could clearly hear what they were saying. The unfortunate young man was apparently proposing to leave him for work on television and Atkins was lecturing him on the professional and moral dangers inherent in such a course of action. Two hours later I returned to the church to find he was still there haranguing his unfortunate victim!

It was the open auditions, however, that were the real horror. They were usually announced in The Stage, the industry's trade paper, but word of mouth could also swiftly circulate the news that one was taking place. If they were for a major production, or were being arranged by a well-known production management the queues would start hours before the stated time. I attended one being held at the Drury Lane theatre for the production of a new musical. I arrived early, but already an unruly throng of aspiring artistes was being denied entry through the stage door. With some difficulty an official managed to get us to form an orderly queue and from that we were admitted in small groups, with much pushing and shoving among those who thought they should be ahead of others.

When I eventually arrived backstage in this famous venue I learnt that we were required to sing "If I Loved You" from the musical "Carousel". Fortunately it was in my repertoire and I felt more hopeful. After a wait that seemed like hours and probably was I found myself on the huge stage, blinded by spot lights. There was a pianist in the orchestra pit and beyond him I could just make out a small group in the front stalls. Someone called out to ask for my name. I gave it and was told that I had to sing "If I Loved You", but starting with the high note on the line: "Longing to Tell You", I got as far as: "I'd let my golden chances...", when the voice from the stalls shouted: "thank you", and that was the outcome of several hours' torture

On another occasion I answered an advertisement for a singer/character actor in what was described as "a summer show" being produced during the holiday season in an East Anglian seaside resort. The audition was held in a Soho rehearsal studio. There was only a small queue on the steps up to the first floor and in no time I was admitted to the tiny room. Asked what I proposed to perform I announced that I would sing "Sea Fever", by John Ireland. It was a song I had been practising with my coach and I was quite pleased with it. I handed my music to the accompanist and began. Somewhat to my surprise they allowed me to get through two verses, then I was stopped by one of the auditors. He picked up my music and examined it with curiosity and respect. Then he complimented me on my rendering, but asked:: did I not realise the audition was for a cowboy show? I was not offered the job.

One other advantage in attending auditions was that before the days of the internet, mobile phones and the rest, it served as an instant communication link with fellow sufferers. One often received links to potential work or at least learnt the latest news in this ever changing industry. One day I was chatting up two young actresses who told me of an exciting new venture in which they were about to be involved. A group had been formed by a man named Bryan Way, who was promoting new and revolutionary ideas about acting and organised regular gatherings at which they could be practised with exercises. The techniques he was proposing involved improvisation and would, he believed, revolutionise the whole business of acting.

I realised they were referring to the Method, a system of training actors that had originated in the USA. It was initiated in the Actors Studio run by Lee Strasbourg in New York. He had taken the teaching of Stanislavski, added a helping of Freud and Jung, and tried to apply it to the American stage. Obviously the system is too complicated to describe in detail here, but basically it involved the actor absorbing the nature of the character he or she was playing through a mental process rather than approaching it technically by learning lines and obeying stage directions.

There had been resistance to it in the UK, particularly from drama academies, such as RADA and LAMDA, who were obviously not going to accept techniques that might be contrary to their own systems of training. The professional theatre was dominated by established stars and family hierarchies that also regarded new ideas as a possible threat.

In the States famous film stars, including Marlon Brando and Dustin Hoffman, claimed they had used "the system" in their own work with considerable success. But that was on film. Those who attempted to apply it in the theatre came up against certain obstacles. The first of these was the necessity to learn lines. Then instead of a close-up camera they had to interpret and communicate in a satisfactory manner to a live audience. In a film studio. If actors forgot their lines there would be retakes. Far from having to express an emotion to an audience of several thousand people, all they had to do was to maintain an expressionless face and let the lighting and camera do the rest.

There is a story that Dustin Hoffman spent three days and nights without sleep in order to get into his part. He related this to his co-star Laurence Olivier, who remarked: "Why didn't you just act". James Cagney, on the other hand, one of the older school, is on record as giving the following advice to an aspiring actor: "Learn your lines; plant your feet; look the camera in the eye; say the words; mean them".

It appeared that Brian Way had become something of a

disciple for these new techniques. I never did discover whether he had been an actor himself, or what experience he had received in the professional theatre, but he obviously saw himself as a teacher and I was not sure whether he had anything to pass on to me that I had not already gained from my admittedly limited experience. So when these young ladies asked me to attend one of the group's meetings I initially declined.

Then they told me he was also a playwright and director and was organising what were known as "schools tours". This was a very different prospect. The idea of playing to young and impressionable audiences was appealing. I gathered that the productions, although presented in school halls, were organised on a professional basis and actors were paid the going Equity rates. It was worth exploring at least. So I agreed to go along.

The meeting was held in a hall in St John's Wood and when I arrived with my two new acquaintances it was in semi-darkness. A radiogram was playing Sibelius. Dim forms were making their way round the hall, more or less silently, performing rudimentary dance steps and making various gestures. We stood at the side and watched, baffled. A female figure threw itself down on to the floor at our feet. One of my companions jumped back in mock alarm, then moved to help, but it got up and continued its convoluted journey.

After a while the music ended and the participants collapsed in various attitudes on the floor. The lights were switched on and they made their way to chairs positioned around the hall, where they sat in postures of inertia or perhaps contemplation. A youngish bearded man who seemed to be in charge came up to us and greeted my two companions by kissing each on the cheek. They introduced him to me as Brian Way, he looked at me very keenly and said: "You are interested in the method". It should have been a question, but he made it sound like an assertion.

An essential element in the new method was improvisation - another technique that had yet to make an impact in the UK. So when the group had recovered from their exertions he called out something I thought was rather curious: "All right Norman. Start a play".

A short, moustachioed young man readily stood up and went to sit on a rostrum in the centre of the room. Placing his chin on one hand and an elbow on his knee he sat there for what seemed to me like quite a long time, until Brian said: "Well, for heaven's sake, someone take pity on him". A young woman went to sit by him and started a conversation. They were joined by others and the group eventually became quite animated. This seemed to please Brian, who applauded and encouraged them.

This kind of exercise was repeated a number of times during my visits to the group and to me had a serious flaw. Basically it lacked any kind of form. The "plays" the participants were supposed to be creating were often set in a kind of no-man's-land, a purgatorial situation that never developed satisfactorily. I decided that this was because there was no scenario, no canvas on to which the participants could apply their verbal paint. Even a jazz instrumentalist requires a basic theme on which to extemporise.

I began to think I was wasting my time when it was announced that a tour had been arranged to play at schools in a county outside London. There were no auditions and somewhat to my surprise I was offered what I suppose could be regarded as the leading part. The play was written by Brian and I was interested to note that, for all his belief in the value of improvisation, when it came to performance before an audience – even children – it was still necessary to have a script.

The play was called The Stranger, after the leading character, which I played. It involved appearing through a bookcase to give a key to a young person (I cannot remember exactly why). There were then lots of antics involving characters and animals from various children's stories. For example, at some point I divested myself of my robe and hood and reappeared as Dr Doolittle. I am not sure whether this practice involved any infringement of copyright.

We travelled in a converted van with the scenery, which comprised a rostrum, some scaffolding and a bookcase with artificial books. Arrived at a school, we were greeted with varying degrees of enthusiasm by members of the staff and set our little stage up in the assembly hall. I found the children wonderful to play to, sometimes finding myself engaging the attention of a particular child and watching as the expression on his or her face turned to wonder and enchantment. Teachers were often less impressed. I noticed that one sat in the middle of the audience marking exercise books - not, I thought, a very good example to her charges. At one point we had to encourage the children to run around the hall searching for the lost key. The teachers would stare in panic and seemed amazed when we had no difficulty in quietening the children, returning them to their seats and regaining their attention.

The other members of the cast were younger than me, obviously inexperienced and some of them acting professionally for the first time. At one point in the run, they seemed to lose concentration during the play, fluffing their lines and not fully engaging the attention of the children. Before performances, under the influence of Brian's training, they would congregate in the equivalent of backstage and think themselves into their parts, eschewing all outside influences in case it disturbed their concentration. One evening I decided to do something about it with a little experiment. Instead of quietly tolerating the situation I told them jokes and made them laugh despite themselves. They were dismayed at my antics and feared they would go on and forget their lines. In fact their performances improved and we had no further trouble

The young lady who played the lead in the school production was very pretty, with long dark hair and deep brown eyes. One night in our provincial digs I spent an hour or two in her room having a drink after the show. She was wearing a very skimpy nightgown. We talked theatre and after a while she announced her intention of going to bed and did so. I stood over her to say good night. I looked down at her, with her hair spread across the pillow. She was very desirable so I bent and kissed her gently. She returned the kiss and obviously would not have objected if I had joined her in bed. She was very young and engaged to be married. I was the senior member of the company. It was the kind of situation that many men of my age presumably experience. I felt I had a certain responsibility in the matter and desisted. I told her I did not want to become her slave, which she took with surprise but philosophically.

A couple of days later in the course of our play, I emerged from behind the bookcase and held my hand out for the key she was supposed to give me. Instead of doing so she collapsed quite dramatically. She was unable to account for what had happened and suggested that she was perhaps over-tired. Brian Way arranged for her to be replaced. A young man arrived in a car to take her away and it appeared she was pregnant. The two seemed to be very much in love and I felt gratified that I had not done anything to disturb their conjugal bliss.

I enjoyed my tour with the children's theatre. It taught me something about children and audience participation. I had no wish to repeat the experience, however, and when it was over I think Brian Way was quite relieved to be able to replace me with someone who regarded his teaching with greater credibility. I had a short break at home and was soon involved in something that, such is the nature of the theatre, could not have been more different.

Chapter 23 - Camper than the campers

The national pastime of taking an annual holiday was something that had passed me by, but I had read about the popular phenomenon of the holiday camp, best known of which was Butlins. These offered holidaymakers a total experience, comprising all meals, refreshments, accommodation and various forms of entertainment. The camps boasted no less than three theatres, the largest showing major musical productions, a smaller one for general purposes and a "repertory theatre". This was repertory in the true sense of the word, offering a "repertoire" of different plays every night so that, if they wished, holiday makers could see all of them during a week's stay. The programme was then repeated every week.

Butlins contracted out the production of the plays to a concessionary company, the Forbes Russell Theatre Company, which presented the same programme at all the camps, using the same scripts and similar scenery. The latest camp to be opened was in the south coast seaside resort of Bognor Regis and I was engaged as the director and to play a number of leading and smaller parts.

We presented four plays during the week, each of them condensed to an hour's length, the theory being that happy campers could not be expected to remain in one place for any longer! There was no interval as it was feared that, if they left their seats for any reason, they would not return for the rest of the play. Presumably the adaptations were with the agreement of the playwrights and, indeed, were sometimes written by them. They were typical repertory fare: A Shred of Evidence, by R. C. Sherriff; Roar Like a Dove, by Lesley Storm; Happy the Bride, (formerly Mock Orange) by Peter Blackmore; and The Last Word, by Jack Popplewell.

The head office laid down the specifications for production and presentation, to which companies in all the camps were expected to conform. This was applied strictly, which I thought was unnecessarily bureaucratic. I tended to modify the dialogue if I thought it could be improved and adapted the stage set-up in the light of practical experience. The ground plan of one play, for example, required a door centre stage. Because the scenery was unstable this caused problems every time it was used so I substituted an archway, which improved the smooth running of the play, but caused consternation when a representative from head office visited to see if we were behaving ourselves!

At the beginning of the season, during a two weeks' rehearsal and pre-production period, we stayed on the camp, sleeping in the tiny chalets that would later be occupied by holiday makers and eating typical camp food. During the season there was plenty of time to observe the campers and see how they enjoyed themselves. I was amused to see how they were not allowed to sit quietly in a deck chair and read, but were coerced and even bullied into participating in various activities, such as bingo, picking apples out of a barrel with their teeth, and nobbly knee competitions.

Fortunately, as we were employed by the theatre company and not by Butlin's after the initial period we stayed off camp and I found accommodation in digs at a village just outside the town. This sometimes created an impasse with the "security" guards on the gates who did not like to see personnel leaving the camp without identifying themselves! I was once held up for quite a time arguing with a guard who seemed intent in restricting the right of an Englishman to freedom.

The situation may be different today, but this kind of approach did not improve the reputation of holiday camps, although they obviously offered value for money and provided many families with holidays they may not otherwise have afforded. There was a small theatre on the promenade in Bognor, presenting nightly revues. One of the principal comic's regular jokes was to add while asking audiences to encourage their friends and acquaintances to attend: "and if you know anyone on the Butlin's camp, let us know and we will organise an escape party,!" This was generally received with delighted laughter and cheers.

The auditorium in our theatre seated nearly 2,000 on one long raked level so that it was like playing to a crowded underground station. We tried to persuade ourselves that we were offering a degree of sanity in the unreal Butlin environment, but the camp was always in danger of intruding. Near the stage was a notice board, with a light over it and the words "A baby is crying in chalet number –". With total disregard for what was transpiring on the stage a camp attendant would enter from the rear, march down the centre aisle, go up to the notice board, insert a number, and flick the light on and off. Somewhere in the audience parents would leave their seats, disturb their neighbours (they always seemed to be in the middle of a row) and leave.

The attendants who performed this task were, of course, the Redcoats, who would take any opportunity to "play to the audience", even when summoning parents to their recalcitrant charges. On one occasion I was in my dressing room prior to appearing on stage in a murder mystery. I had a small part in this play and was despatched by a gunshot early in the action. It was important to build up tension in the audience from the beginning. While I was putting on my make-up I heard gales of laughter coming from the auditorium. I sent an assistant stage manager to find out what was happening and she returned with the news that we had been invaded by a Redcoat who was on stage entertaining the audience. Backstage staff did their best to call him off but he refused to go and even made fun of their attempts to stop him, telling the audience that "these stuffy old actors" were only jealous of the Redcoats' popularity. I complained to camp management afterwards, but was informed that he was only doing his job as it was the camp's policy not to allow any audience to sit quietly without being entertained!

One would have expected that our little theatre company would be a happy group of performers, something like Priestley's Good Companions. Nothing, however, could have been further from the truth. From the outset our two heavy leading men (one of them the company manager) made it clear that they regarded themselves as a class apart from the rest. They claimed the largest dressing room for the pair of them and would remain closeted there until required on stage or it was time to leave the theatre. They also developed an antipathy towards the two young "juvenile leads", who happened to be husband and wife.

The stage manager was a tall slim young man who made his sexual preferences plain from the start and quickly established a rapport with the two heavies. One of the ASMs was a teen-aged lad, who came to me one day almost in tears. Could I give him advice? What was he to do? He was being urged to accept the idea that he was homosexual. I told him he should follow his own predilections, but he said he was not sure what they were. How could I advise him? I suggested he should confide in the other ASM, who was a pretty young woman, a little older, but rather more mature. I never knew whether or not he took my advice, or if he did what the effect was, but I noticed that he began to appear happier and more relaxed as he went about his work!

It was a pleasant enough period of my life spending my time between the cloistered world of the camp, the village I lived in and the relaxed atmosphere of a seaside resort in summer. I was unaware of the outside world and did not at first realise how isolated I had become. This came home to me one day when I was standing at the bus stop on my way to the camp. A worried-looking young lady obviously decided I was the kind of sympathetic person she could confide in. She remarked how awful the crisis was. I asked her "what crisis". She looked at me in astonishment. "Why, Nigeria, of course". Having not read a newspaper for months, I had been totally unaware of it.

Another important aspect of life was in danger of passing me by. I had always been keenly interested in music, but that meant anything from Bach to Elgar. I had enjoyed the "big bands" of my youth, but found little sympathy with the modern involvement in "pop" or "rock and roll". During the season a young man named Jeff came to stay in at the digs who was the lead guitarist and vocalist for a pop group playing daily in Bognor's little promenade theatre. I enjoyed chatting to him, usually over breakfast, and one day he suggested I should go to hear him play at one of his regular afternoon concerts. It seemed ungracious of me to refuse and I went along expecting to be out of place in an audience of teenagers and even children. Instead I was astonished to find myself among middle-aged and elderly people tapping their feet and enjoying a type of music that I thought would only appeal to younger generations.

One morning Jeff joined me for breakfast and asked for my help as he believed I knew something about music. I suggested that my knowledge was probably more limited than his, but he produced a copy of the first and most basic primer and turned to page 1. He said he was puzzled about what were called bar signatures. He knew about 4/4, but what were 3/4 and 6/8? I was astonished. I had seen him play the guitar at the concert and he seemed to know what he was doing. How could he lead a musical group when he not only had no musical knowledge, but was unable even to understand it when it was presented in a book? He explained that all he had to do was to follow the chords indicated at the top of the staves and place his fingers on the correct guitar frets. Later he visited my theatre on the camp. On stage he looked around and asked: "Where are the microphones?" I said we did not use them. Astonished, he exclaimed: "But how do you make yourself heard?" That was something I was not going to try and explain.

Like all summer seasons it came to an end at last and I returned to London to endure one of those thin periods of unemployment experienced by many who work in the professional theatre. In order to maintain some activity on stage whatever form it took I became involved in a semi-professional company presenting shows in the London parks, on band-stands and other outdoor venues. The producer was an aspiring comic named Warwick Price and the "star" of the show former opera singer Joan Colyer. It was a surprisingly large company and I do not think anyone was paid very much, if anything at all. They took me on as resident male singer and "straight" man in the comedy sketches.

Rehearsals were almost non-existent. Warwick would explain the basic business and outline the dialogue, which depended to some extent on his improvisation. He suggested I wore a jacket that would not be spoilt if it got wet. I assumed this was in case it rained, but the first time we did it I found the reason was he spewed a mouthful of water over me to get a laugh. One of my solos was "A Pretty Girl is like a Melody", during which I was joined by a couple of pretty young female members of the group. Suddenly the audience started howling with laughter. I was bewildered. Were my flies undone? Was my singing that bad? Then I realised Warwick had entered dressed in outrageous drag.

One day I had a curiously enlightening experience. I was singing a song I knew particularly well and had the feeling I had left my body and was hovering above it controlling myself like a puppet. My voice seemed to be projected without any apparent effort on my part. I cannot explain this and can only say it happened. I'm sure the experience is not unique.

During this time I had my first and only experience of the film industry. A call went out for actors to take part in crowd voice-overs for a film entitled Khartoum, based on the death of General Gordon. It was a day's work and I was curious to see what life was like in a film studio, which turned out to be Pinewood. About 30 of us assembled in the room and were shown clips of the action on a large screen. We were expected to shout alla akaba as the Mahdi's men charged across the desert in a battle. We did for a morning, then broke for lunch. When we reassembled it transpired that what we had been calling was wrong. It was corrected and we went through it again. Then there was an attack at the walls of a castle. Someone was shown falling from the ramparts. The director asked if any of us could scream. I put my hand up and, surprisingly, seemed to be the only one. So the shot was played and I screamed. Then it was shown again, several times, and each time I provided the sound track. It may not be much, but at least on my list of credits I can say I was a scream in Khartoum.

Chapter 24 – A wandering minstrel

A form of theatrical activity providing a useful source of experience and income for the actor was the provincial tour. This was a tradition that had obviously existed for hundreds of years as Shakespeare himself was probably introduced to the professional theatre when he joined a company of actors travelling on carts from market town to market town. One recalls the excited anticipation with which the strolling players were greeted in the court where Hamlet plotted his revenge. I joined one such company, although we neither travelled nor performed on a cart and the reception was sometimes less enthusiastic than in Shakespeare's day, but at least we did not have to deal with a wild-eyed prince telling us what play we had to perform!

I toured with a little piece called Hot and Cold in All Rooms, the cultural level of which was approximately that of the Carry On films, with dialogue resembling "Are you being served", the popular sit-com of later TV years, but without its ascorbic wit! It was set in what was described as a "good class Kensington apartment house", among the occupants of which were several young ladies anxious to acquire suitable mates. The announcement that they were to be joined by a personable young man created a flutter in their amorous hearts. To their dismay, when he arrived it transpired he was the sort of flamboyant male, with the name of Cecil, who prefers the company of other men to that of women. It would not go down well with modern audiences, but at the time it was one of the most popular plays both in rep. and on the circuit.

My agent arranged an appointment with the producer and he took me on without even asking me to audition. Somewhat to my surprise, he offered me the part of Cecil. I pointed out not only was I not homosexual, but did not have the appearance usually attributed at that time to those with the character's sexual proclivities. He insisted, however, that being "butch" was an advantage. He suggested it removed the possibility of causing any offence and for me would be a challenge. It was certainly that!

I was not entirely convinced by his arguments, or that I could carry it off, but it was work and I was not going to turn it down, In the event it was not a total disaster. Indeed, the audience seemed to enjoy it. The key to success or otherwise for me lay in my entrance. I had to poke my head round the door and say one word: "Hullo!". If it got a laugh then I felt I was on safe comic ground. Among the theatres we played were the New, Kingston-upon-Hull; the Empire, Newcastle; and the Theatre Royal, Bath. I still have press cuttings of reviews that appeared in the local papers, which did not rate the play very highly, but were kind towards my performance.

On another tour I was stage director as well as acting in a character part. The play was The Death Is Announced, in which the leading part was played by Reginald Marsh, who was later frequently to be seen on television. I disliked touring as a stage director. The responsibility for moving the play successfully from theatre to theatre and town to town fell solely, and heavily, on my shoulders. Waiting outside a stage door at midnight for transport to take the scenery and props. to the next destination could be particularly stressful, bearing in mind that the whole enterprise depended on it and at that time of night, on a Saturday, in a strange town there would be no fall-back if the truck failed to appear.

There was also the question of dealing with the crew when I arrived at the next date. They would be responsible for building the set beforehand and for any scene changes during the run and it was important for me to establish my authority, without being autocratic. I found that if I turned up scruffily dressed in sweater and jeans I was treated with less respect than if I wore in a suit and tie, when possibly my clothes identified me as the person responsible for handing out gratuities! It also helped if they felt I was experienced backstage and not simply somebody down from the office. On one occasion I was backstage while they were putting the main set together. A stage hand had put a 20-foot flat into position beside another and was preparing to "throw the cleat". He looked at me, smiled and offered the rope. I smiled back, took it and without looking up, gave it a twirl so that it landed in position with a satisfying clunk. He was suitably impressed and I had no trouble with that crew!

On another occasion I almost gave the star of the show a heart-attack. A hand gun had to be fired on stage and it was always my practice to check its efficacy before the show. I did this back stage at the top of the concrete stairs leading past the dressing rooms, unaware that Reginald was talking to somebody by the stage door. In those surroundings the noise was deafening. There a long silence after which Reginald's pale face appeared around the corner of the landing. "Thank you Leslie", he said quietly. "I feel better now!"

I also appeared in what were known as "special weeks" in established rep. companies. At the Grand Theatre, Wolverhampton, for example, I played the lead in Gilt and Gingerbread, a light comedy by well-known actor, Lionel Hale. I was then invited back later to play the inspector in Agatha Christie's Verdict. This attracted full houses every night. All the rep. theatres knew that, if they were having a bad season, they only needed to offer an Agatha Christie to recoup some of their losses.

I had a small part as a uniformed policeman at the Richmond Theatre, Bath. It was memorable because the rather unpleasant leading man seemed to take a dislike to me and tried to ruin one of my short scenes. At a dramatic moment I had to burst through a door and arrest someone. It was important that the last person through the door, who happened to be this actor, should leave it off the latch, otherwise I risked knocking half the set down. I noticed, however, on one night he latched it, possibly on purpose. Fortunately, having seen him, I was able to turn the handle as I burst through.

Most of this work came through my agent, a firm which went by the name of Guy Charles, although it was under the management of his wife Mary Leigh. In addition to placing artistes in employment she ran a theatre production company, producing summer seasons in a number of seaside towns. These were popular with actors at all stages of their careers as they offered reasonably well-paid employment in congenial surroundings. If the weather was good they could learn their lines while sun-bathing on a beach. Audiences were receptive and pleasant to play to as they were generally in holiday mood.

One of Mary's seasons was in Bognor Regis, Sussex; another in Minehead, Somerset. She appointed me as director and leading actor with the arrangement that I would direct and appear in the first three productions in Bognor, then for the rest of the season move with some of the cast to Minehead, which started three weeks later.

In Bognor the tiny theatre was at the land end of the pier. One could see the water between the floor boards of the dressing rooms! The plays were mainly run-of-the-mill repertory fare, such as Birthday Honours, by Paul Jones, and A Sound of Murder, by William Fairchild. Rather more ambitious with its costumes and changes of scenery was Gigi in the stage version I had worked on earlier as an electrician in the West End.

The Queen's Theatre in Minehead was rather more salubrious, pleasantly located on the sea front. During morning rehearsals we would hear a distant horn and break off to go on to a balcony overlooking the promenade. A coach and four would drive by with its complement of holiday makers, the driver and postilions in period dress and a pair of coach dogs (Dalmatians) trotting by its side .We would exchange waves with the passengers, which would be good publicity for our shows. The coach and horses were located in an old coaching inn at the far end of town. The owner, who drove the coach, was a flamboyant character, tall and immensely handsome, whose father, it was rumoured, had been a Bengal Lancer! He was also an amateur actor, with a huge voice, who would sometimes be drafted into the cast, although I am not sure if Equity would have approved.

The local residents obviously enjoyed having a professional theatre company during what was quite a long summer season. They were very hospitable, would stop us in the street and comment on the latest performance. There was a fishmonger in the High Street who would wrap up a lobster or brace of haddock and hand them to us with a few words of appreciation as we passed. Village people and farmers would come regularly from miles around, including a blacksmith who came every week, always occupying the same seat in the front stalls.

As with Bognor, we played the usual repertory fare of murder mysteries and comedies, something perhaps not all that different from what is watched nowadays so avidly by millions of people on television. The scenery was makeshift, the actors poorly paid, the management obviously on the tightest of budgets, yet between us we were managing to keep the theatre alive. Sadly, when I returned to Minehead some years later on other business I found the little Queens Theatre had gone the way of so many of its fellows and had become an amusement arcade.

Needless to say this constant travelling and playing at different venues made it very difficult for me to enjoy much time with my wife and children. I suppose my own family background had led me not to expect too much in the way of conjugal bliss, but whatever I was doing I did try to ensure that they were well looked after. My wife was a good mother and we were all fortunate in that my mother had the opportunity to be involved in and care for a family that was perhaps happier than her own.

My absences were probably no worse than those experienced by many men who find themselves in a transitory existence. Had I remained a merchant seaman, for example, I could have been overseas for months at a time. Sadly, however, there is no doubt that my relationship with my wife became increasingly strained. Inevitably there was a widening divergence in our lives, due also to the inevitable changes that take place in the thoughts and outlooks of a couple with the passing years. We had met, after all, when I was a merchant seaman and she a waitress. The likelihood of our lives progressing along similar paths was remote. It is sad, but young love seldom lasts. Perhaps it is little more than the fantasy of the romance writers or Hollywood. Whatever the truth of the matter, circumstances were about to put our relationship to the test.

Chapter 25 - "We'll be in love by the end of the season"

My next summer season was as a leading actor in the quite superior Prince of Wales theatre in Colwyn Bay, North Wales, I was booked to join the company with their second play in the season, so that I arrived on the opening night of the first one. Rehearsals for my play began the next day and I was handed a script for the first time. It was called The Vanity Case, written by Jack Popplewell, an author whose work I had encountered before and who was, I understand, a High Court judge. Personally I thought he deserved a lengthy sentence for having inflicted such a play on a long suffering actor.

The curtain rose to an empty stage. The doors at the back opened and most of the cast entered into what was the typical middle class living room setting of the average repertory thriller. I followed them on in the role of a police inspector investigating a murder. I began asking questions and continued to do so for three acts! Playing a detective on stage presents one special difficulty: the nature of his role means that most of his dialogue is in the form of leading questions,which means he gets little in the way of helpful cues from the other characters.

I had 72 pages to learn in a week! Fortunately I had a reasonably retentive memory and I used two techniques to assist me. One of these was known as the "brown envelope" system used by many actors. It involved moving a brown envelope (for some reason it was always an envelope and usually brown) down a page giving the cue for the next line. The other was to lie in bed first thing in the morning and try to go through the whole part without reference to the script. If I could do that by the Saturday I reckoned I knew it.

In the case of the Vanity Case, despite my hard work and experience I almost had a disaster on the opening night. Halfway through the first act I was required to send the rest of the cast off stage, telling them I would interview them one by one. I was thus left alone on stage with nothing between me and the audience. At this point I had my first and only serious "dry" on stage, which as all actors know resembles a kind of mental blackout. I realised I had not the slightest idea what was to come next. There I was on an empty stage, with an audience watching my every move. The play and perhaps the whole season depended on my recovering my memory. I decided that as everyone else had left the stage I had better follow them.

I walked off into what fortunately was the "prompt" side of the stage. There I shouted the word "prompt" to the assistant stage manager in the corner, who was fortunately on the ball and responded with the one word "Spinks". This was the name of my constable and immediately brought me back on track. I strolled on to the stage purposefully as if my leaving had been part of the plot and said "Come in here for a minute, will you Spinks". From then on I was in command.

Despite the relatively high standard of presentation we did have one typically hilarious property mishap on the opening night of a musical play called "Meet me By Moonlight", which had a modest run on the West End. It incorporated Victorian songs into a tale of romance and as I could sing was given the romantic leading part. I preceded my entrance singing a romantic song off stage, which I continued as I swept into the room wearing a cloak and hat.

The heroine was playing the piano and when the song was over she stood and I was supposed to greet her by plucking a rose from a vase positioned on the piano and presenting it to her with the words, "a rose to a rose". What I did not know was that during dress rehearsal the director felt that the tall vase of artificial flowers obscured the actress playing the piano. An enterprising stage manager had, therefore, twisted their stems into a shape that could be accommodated in a bowl. So that when I lifted my floral tribute with a flourish the whole lump came out like a cabbage!

The theatre director was Maurice Jones, who also played character parts in some of the plays. He was an actor of the old school, keen on the use of make-up, wigs and facial hair. Unlike most actors, he used water-based face paint, mixing his colours in little jars on his dressing table. (Later this became more common when it was feared that the oil-based make-up adversely affected the skin.)

When I was offered the part I expressed concern about my age and thinning hair. Could I have a wig? Maurice was against this, largely I believe because of the cost of hiring. He also insisted that I should wear large curved sideboards, which he offered me from his make-up store. I hated them. When I looked in the mirror on the opening night I thought it was grotesque. Then I found that they effectively covered my bald patch and I was able to devise smaller sideboards from crepe hair. After the show Maurice expressed his satisfaction at the success of his sideboards and also reassured me that my bald patch did not show at all. I did not enlighten him!

This was a long season, running for 18 weeks from the beginning of June to the beginning of October. The programme comprised the usual repertory fare. Plays by Agatha Christie always drew the largest audiences, one of them – Verdict - being revived from last year. The rest were mainly thrillers and light comedies. Exceptions were old work horses like The Shop at Sly Corner, The Cat and the Canary and Priestley's Mr Kettle and Mrs Moon.

It was a very special time for me as I was able to concentrate on acting without the distraction of direction or stage management. It was as if, after a long period of engagement, I had at last entered into a formal partnership with a profession I had grown to love. There was another aspect of my time in Colwyn Bay that paralleled my affair with the theatre and gave it an additional romantic glow.

The leading lady in the company was an actress whom I will call Veronica. She was not beautiful in the traditional sense of the word, but had the attractiveness that comes from a strong personality, good intellect and, perhaps more significant than anything, sexual magnetism. She had fair hair and blue eyes. Her nose was aquiline rather than retrousé. Her figure was slight, but well formed. One day I was in the High Street of the town and I saw her walking along on the opposite side of the road. I do not think she saw me and I watched as she went along, her head held high, her coat open as she braved the breeze coming off the sea. There was something about her, about the way she held her head, about what seemed to be her courage in confronting whatever fate held for her. I suppose I was falling in love.

She was married to an actor she had not seen for months. They shared a flat in Clapham, but he was under long-term contract to a provincial theatre. At the end of our season she would be returning to an empty home. I also would be returning home, but in my case would have to face my wife and family. In such a way are marriages in the theatrical and film world broken, however bravely they are embarked upon and however meaningful the vows that are made.

Because of our work we were thrown together constantly and found we had a great deal in common, in our reading, intellectual excitements and aspirations. Then, there was the excitement of working together on stage, the rapport that arose from rehearsals, from learning together during hot, sunny hours spent on the beach or in the rooms at our digs. I was a long way from home. I had been spending more time away from my wife and family than with them. What followed, I suppose was inevitable.

Even through the disguise of our stage personae we would find someone we were beginning to love beneath the make-up. In Billy Liar we had to play the mother and father. Her hair was greyed and she had wrinkles made up around her eyes and mouth. I was also supposed to be older, sporting a very unattractive moustache. Yet as we stood at the side of the stage, waiting to go on, we looked through the masquerade and smiled at the unreality of the situation. So much for method acting!

One afternoon there was an opportunity to attend a matinee at a theatre in a nearby town. They were presenting Salad Days, which neither of us had seen. It is a flimsy, but charming piece. The young couple on stage sang: "We'll be in love by the end of the season". Veronica and I allowed the romance of the occasion to immerse us. We clasped hands and looked at one another. I thought: "We are already" and I am sure she thought so too.

Chapter 26 – Back to the smoke

The season in Colwyn Bay came to an end and Veronica and I went back in London, the London I loved, my fiefdom. This was the late 1960s, however, the world was changing dramatically and London with it. I was determined to stay in town as long as I could and now I had an additional incentive to hold me there. Veronica was living alone in her flat in Clapham and our relationship deepened.

She received a commission to translate from the French several volumes in a series of about 20 books on art. We worked together on six of them, including those on Dutch, Japanese and modern painting. She produced the basic translations and I edited and put them into acceptable prose. She showed me how to solve cryptic crosswords, which she liked to do before going to sleep at night. On a more practical level, she taught me how to cook spaghetti Bolognese, the staple dish for all itinerants.

My wife obviously realised something was wrong and challenged me about it. I like to think I am a truthful person and found it impossible to lie. I hoped that by being honest we could find some way of getting through the situation. After all, affairs of this kind, however intense, do not always last and it was important to maintain the family unit if at all possible. I suppose I was expecting too much and her reaction was predictable.

Living at the old house was also something I found difficult. There had been so much distress there, so many years of emotional turmoil. The crumbling old building was a metaphor for the struggles that had taken place during my upbringing. With the help of my son Graham I tried to repair the ravages the years had wrought on the Victorian lath-and-plaster-work, only to find the gaps widening. They were like cancerous growths that only became worse from the application of medication. I felt its oppressiveness like a curse.

My presence seemed only to act as an additional irritation to Doris and I felt she and the children would be better off without me. I had, after all, spent many periods working and living away from home and my absences were something they were used to. I loved them dearly. Wendy and my other daughter Maxine were beautiful girls and Graham was growing up to be a happy, practical young man. I was not looking to neglect them and hope I never did emotionally or financially. My mother would still live with them and seemed to find a kind of rejuvenation in helping to care for a new family.

I found a little room in Beauchamp Place, just off Knightsbridge. It seems amazing now that I was able to afford even a small room in that area of London, located immediately behind Harrods. It was an exciting experience being able to walk out of my front door and immediately into the swirl of London life. A disadvantage was that it comprised only half a room, with a light, hardboard partition dividing the two apartments. The other half was occupied by an elderly lady, who must have found her neighbour a great irritation. She complained about the noise of my typewriter and when Veronica came to visit, as she did quite frequently, would hammer on the wall and shout invectives.

About this time I was cast in a couple of parts on television, which I had not worked in since "Crossroads". One was a play called "Breaking Point", in which I played the part of a bank guard; the other was an episode in a popular series called "The Troubleshooters", which had a distinguished cast, including Robert Hardy and Geoffrey Keene. I disliked the work, finding it technical and unrewarding. It seemed to me that the actors had very little say in the process of production, or even in the way they played their parts. Despite the considerable skill of the actors what finishes up on the TV screens depends on the decisions of the director, the ability of the cameramen and the appropriateness of the lighting.

But it paid the rent and provided me with an insight

into the way these productions were put together. I learnt that having decided on the basic theme for the project various writers would be commissioned to provide individual episodes. This would mean that the script was sometimes accepted regardless of quality. By a coincidence I was invited to a party in Hampstead attended by the joint writers of the episode in which I was appearing. Very well-known scriptwriters for both TV and film, they were boasting how they would produce 10,000 words in a day.

A few days later at the studio I attended a meeting comprising the directors, leading actors and other cast members. It was agreed that whole sections of the script were unusable and had to be revised, which we proceeded to do. This process made me really quite angry. It had obviously been thrown together, with little attempt to edit. The writers were paid very good money for their 10,000 words a day and it was then left to the actors and director to do their work for them

So it was with some relief I had the opportunity to return to the live theatre as production manager at The London Traverse Theatre, housed in the Jeanetta Cochran theatre in Holborn. The Edinburgh Traverse had achieved fame as the first theatre with a stage in the middle of the audience. It has been suggested that the word should have been Transverse, but as it was already in production the decision was made to retain it.

The intention from the start was to challenge modern mores and conceptions with the presentation of controversial plays. It had been very successful in Edinburgh and it was decided to try and replicate it in London. One of its directors, Michael Geliot moved down to head it up, joined later by Charles Marovitz and Jim Haynes. Haynes was creator and editor of an "underground" newspaper initially entitled International Times, which was changed to IT when the Times Newspaper threatened legal action for infringement of copyright. My work would not involve acting, but I had an interest in the project because it would introduce me to the controversial *avant garde* developments taking place not only in the theatre, but in society generally.

Those involved soon discovered that the Jeanetta Cochrane was a very different animal from the Edinburgh venue. Organisationally and structurally it was part of the London School of Arts and Crafts so that the landlord was the culturally conservative London County Council, which appointed the theatre's manager. As a building it was designed like any other professional theatre and answerable to the same rules and regulations, with a distinct divide between actors and audience and even the legal requirement to lower a fire safety curtain at least once during a performance.

Before I joined the company it did achieve a notable success with Marovitz's production of Joe Orton's "Loot", which transferred successfully to the West End. I remember little or nothing of the plays we produced, except that dramatically they tended to be somewhat obscure. There was inevitably a cultural clash between this new wave of artistic and political activity and the "establishment" and I frequently found myself acting as arbitrator between my directors and the theatre management.

I was also involved in the more difficult task of keeping the enterprise afloat financially. The Theatre's budgeting was casual to say the least. Its principal sponsor was the Arts Council, the director of which at the time was the meritorious Lord Goodman. He was head of a major legal partnership and his various public duties made it very difficult to arrange an appointment with him. I spent many an hour sitting in his reception room hoping for an opportunity to speak to him about the fate of the Traverse. At last I managed to do so and I can recall to this day how he looked at me over his spectacles and complimented me on being the most patient man he had ever had to deal with. He glanced at the budget I showed him and the list of creditors. One of them was apparently a legal firm of his acquaintance. While I was there he telephoned our creditor and reminded him of our debt, ending his conversation with the comment: "You don't expect to get paid do you?"

I personally did not feel that the anarchic element sat easily on the professional theatre, which depends so much on centuries of tradition and the skills and training of all those involved. It is essentially a pact between author, director, actor and scenic designers on the one hand and the audience on the other. The writer can express unusual and even revolutionary ideas, but it must be with the connivance of those who pay to sit, watch and listen.

I did put a toe in the water of modernity by directing a lunch-time production at the little Playroom Theatre in the Swiss Tavern, Old Compton Street. It comprised two plays by the Italian writer Mario Fratti: The Suicide and The Refusal. One of them starred a talented young actor named Robert Cotton. He was then appearing every night naked in the notorious revue "Oh! Calcutta", alongside other members of a cast that included Tony Booth, who later worked on television and was, as most people know, Cheri Blaire's father.

Chapter 27 - Actor manager

Veronica and I took a lease on a first-floor flat in Wimbledon. It was a commodious apartment, in a side road half way up Wimbledon Hill, about a mile away from the Common and the tennis courts and near to a little row of shops. It had a flight of steps up to a porch and its own front door, gardens to the front, side, and back. Such accommodation will be worth a king's ransom nowadays, but it was well within our pockets then.

My mother had died sitting up in a chair before the old-fashioned grate at No. 11, St Michael's Terrace, Wood Green, the house she had lived in for more years than she, or anyone else could remember. My wife was still living in the house with our children and decided to sue for divorce, which passed without rancour. I have to say that at all times she behaved with dignity and perhaps even understanding towards the end. When she moved out I was able to sell the property and use my share of the divorce settlement as part of an initial charge on the lease of my flat.

I acquired a car, a little Austin A35, with an 850cc engine. At the age of 40 it was my first. Up to then it had hardly been necessary to drive in London where the public transport system had been adequate for all my needs. I had to take the driving test and was concerned at the fact that I had spent so little time in cars and certainly never been behind the wheel of one. Somewhat to my surprise I passed first time.

Veronica got work at a summer season in the Lake District and I decided to drive up and visit her, checking with my local garage that the little car would be robust enough for the long journey. I was assured it would. Then Veronica asked me if I would bring up two of the company's actors, who were living in London. It was difficult for me to refuse, so we set out for my first long journey. At that time the M1 ended before the next stretch of motorway began. Still halfway to our destination we were travelling along a stretch of road with only one lane in each direction. On the other side was a continuous line of traffic, which a lorry driver decided to overtake. He was approaching me head on and I was just able to squeeze past him.

Then I made a mistake. Congratulating myself on the skill of my manoeuvre, instead of watching the road ahead I turned to shake a fist at him for endangering the lives of myself and my passengers. Unfortunately the car I had been following stopped and I ran into the back of it. My speed was modest and the other vehicle, a Jaguar, had scarcely a bump. The front of my poor little car caved in and bled green fluid over the road. It was obviously a write-off.

I had a couple of hundred miles to go with two actors due to appear in front of an audience that night. I managed to make contact with a local garage that fortunately had cars for hire. The pick-up truck took me and the car away from the scene, leaving two very dejected actors by the road. The garage owner was very helpful. He disappeared and came back driving a Ford Cortina, which looked to me as big and expensive as a Rolls Royce, bearing in mind the only car I had ever driven was the little Austin and that only for a few months.

He asked me to sign an agreement, which I did. When he looked at it, however, he suggested I had made a mistake by showing the date on which I passed my test as only a few months back. He pointed out that insurers would not cover the driver of a hired car who had been driving less than a year. What was I to do? I hastily "corrected" it and drove away

I then had to face driving the car around the narrow streets of the little town and in excursions into the neighbouring hills, knowing that if anything happened not only would I be responsible for any damage, but had also defrauded the insurance company and would probably spend the next few months of my life in prison. I remember the first thing I did when I got out of bed every morning was to look out of the window to make sure it was still there and had not received any damage during the night. Fortunately there were no mishaps. A few years later I bought my own Cortina and enjoyed it immensely. I returned to London by train and there bought a little Ford Anglia, a car that held the road about as well as a drunken skater on a glacier. I tried to teach Veronica to drive in it, but that was not a happy experience.

A car was now essential to me, however, as I was about to be a frequent traveller to the little town of Henley-on-Thames, Veronica's home town. She told me it possessed one of the oldest theatres in the country – the Kenton – which was sadly under–used. We decided to set up a theatre company to produce plays there. The idea would be to rehearse in London, move to Henley at the week-end for dress rehearsal and then play for a week. We called ourselves the Holborn Theatre Company.

Our first production was to be Bell, Book and Candle, by John Van Druten. This had been a popular play and provided an excellent part as the witch for Veronica. We started rehearsals and things seemed to go well. Veronica had a tendency to play the character with what might be called witch-like characteristics until I suggested that the point of the play was that she did not resemble a witch. I coached her to play it straight, which she did, and she finished up giving a very good performance.

We and the rest of the cast moved down to Henley on the Saturday. The leading actor was a pleasant young man who, at lunch times in London when we would all go for a drink, would excuse himself on the grounds that he wanted to learn his lines on his own. Obviously I approved of this, but when he came on stage at the dress rehearsal in Henley he was obviously drunk. He did not know his lines, or if he did could not speak them. A couple of the cast came to me in the auditorium and told me he had a bottle of vodka in his dressing room. To give the rest of the cast the opportunity to practice I insisted that he staggered through the rest of the play, with the prompter speaking most of his lines.

Then I went to his dressing room and told him to remain on standby. I was going to try and find a replacement. If I could not he would have to go on drunk or sober, but I suggested it was in his best interest to lay off the juice. I travelled up to London and on Monday morning visited the offices of Spotlight, the directory in which all actors had their photos and details, and which also kept a record of productions. I asked them if anyone had played the lead in the play recently. They found that an actor named Simon Oates had in Bromley, a good quality repertory theatre in south London. The trouble was that since appearing there. he had become a major television star, somebody who would nowadays be regarded as a celebrity of the highest standing.

I telephoned him and explained that I wanted someone to step in at the last minute. He agreed and asked how much rehearsal he could have. I told him he was to appear that night, at which the telephone exploded. He demanded to know if it was a practical joke. I told him it was not and that I would be at his office in half an hour with a script. In addition to his acting he ran a successful fashion house just off Regent Street. I went there and to my surprise and great relief he agreed to do it. We set out to drive to Henley and on the way called at his flat in Battersea to pick up some clothes, where I noticed that his wardrobe was probably worth more than my entire production!

Arrived at the theatre, we went in through the front of house to find the cast sitting around miserably on stage, scripts in hands, going through lines and with my character lady fitting cushions into bright new covers. They looked up to see me walk down the aisle with this tall, handsome, glamorous young actor, who to their astonishment and delight I introduced as their new leading man. He came up trumps and at the end of the week was kind enough to say how satisfying he had found the whole experience.

We produced one more play in Henley: Noel Coward's

Private Lives. It went quite well, but the audiences were not good. It was obvious we were not going to make a fortune. We returned to London and Veronica decided she had to accept the offer of work in the provinces, which would mean her living there. I was devastated. I certainly could not continue the company without her. I suspected her of having an affair and, indeed, she did admit to certain indiscretions.

I had lost my business partner, flat sharer and mistress. I believe we really did love one another. For the sake of propriety I have changed her name, but if she happens to read this, either because she is hopefully still alive, or looking down from the nimbus ranks of the angelic hosts, she will know that I remember her and our time together with great respect, pleasure and affection. I was bereft of female companionship. The future, professionally and personally, looked bleak. As so often happens, however, when one is absolutely at the bottom the only way is up. I was about to become involved in the final act of the theatrical drama that had absorbed me for over twenty years. I was bound, at last, for the West End of London.

Chapter 28 – The ultimate goal

It is, I suppose, the dream of all who work in the professional theatre that one day they will reach the West End of London. I had experienced it, of course, but very much in a part-time capacity. Now, my decision to combine acting with stage management was going to pay off. A stage director who could act was a valuable commodity, particularly if he was prepared, as I was, to understudy. One of my boyhood heroes, John Clements, leading actor, film star and theatre director, had joined up with impresario Martin Landau to produce a stage version of C. P. Snow's novel, The Masters. It was to be directed by Clements, with himself playing a leading part. The writer was Ronald Millar, who later became Margaret Thatcher's speech writer. The theatre was to be the Savoy. I was one of two Stage Managers, responsible for the staging, scene changes, etc. My colleague was a young lady who looked after the personal props and ran the prompt corner.

The settings, although apparently simple, were challenging. Unusually, the play was in three acts, each divided into two scenes. Act 1, scene i took place in the "combination" room of a Cambridge University college. In the first scene the furniture comprised a number of heavy leather armchairs and sofas, with oak occasional tables. For the second scene these had to be replaced by a board-room table, with a dozen high-backed Victorian chairs. To make the change, a number of "flats" had to be removed from the scenery on each side of the stage and the furniture moved on and off by a team of some half a dozen stage hands. This took place while the front curtain was down and it was essential that it should be raised as quickly as possible. The tradition for "scene changes" was that the curtain should only have had time to bounce before it was taken up again. During the pre-West End run the change took a minute and a half to achieve.

As the person responsible for ensuring that the change took place as efficiently and rapidly as possible I was called into the presence of the great man, who pointed out that in London if it took so long the audience would probably walk out on the first night. How, I was asked, could it be shortened? I did not have to think for long and told him: "Double the number of stage hands". He agreed and in London did so. The change took place as required.

Modern planners and those responsible for public developments could learn a great deal from the ability of professional theatre producers to fulfil their responsibilities on time, within budget and generally without serious hitches. Putting on a professional theatre production, from the smallest to the largest, does not admit of any mistakes. One cannot turn away a first night audience because the scenery is not ready or the actors have not learnt their lines. In an earlier chapter I recalled Michael Dennison's concern over the position of a pen, after Herculean efforts had been made to revive an Oxford Playhouse production. John Clements was equally meticulous both as a director and an actor. The board table had to be covered by a green baize cloth and each place laid with a blotter and other papers. The blotters were, of course, pasted on to the cloth in advance and I remember how he went round the table during the dress rehearsal with a ruler ensuring that each one was the exact same distance from the edge of the table.

Actors and actresses were needed for an exceptionally large number of characters, including 14 college fellows, a brace of porters and servants. One wonders how the production was expected to make a profit. The cast was not only large in number, but also in years, their ages ranging from 50 to 70. But these were top-class professional performers, some of whom later becoming well-known to television audiences, such as Peter Copley and John Barron.

Sadly, it did not have a long run, but my reputation on the West End was now established and I quickly found another job with a production of Arthur Wing Pinero's "The Schoolmistress", which this time combined understudying with stage management. A popular comedy actor of the time, Nigel Patrick, was in the lead and once again we had a large cast of first class actors, including Charles Heslop and Megs Jenkins, who has since had a very successful television career. We opened in the Theatre Royal, Brighton, and brought the play to the Savoy.

It was a joyous company, largely because Nigel, known to all as Paddy, was a great prankster. To make one entrance he had to walk across the stage behind a large "stage cloth". He found that by swirling his umbrella around on the cloth he could make a sound like an increasing wind, not heard by the audience, but disconcerting the actors on stage.

Then there was a scene in which a small celebratory cake had to be brought on stage and placed on a table. The cast had to stand round it and make comments on what "a very nice cake" it was. On one night Paddy had obtained an imitation dog's turd from a joke shop and placed it on the cake before it was brought on, with the result that the cast had to say their lines with their shoulders shaking from laughter.

The run of The Schoolmistress was also short, but fortunately the team of John Clements and Martin Landau wanted me for an exciting new project. This was to be a major musical based on the play "The Barretts of Wimpole Street", which told the story of the love affair between Robert Browning and Elizabeth Barrett. It was initially entitled "The Barretts and Mr Browning", which was changed to "Robert and Elizabeth".

The book and lyrics were by Ronald Millar, the music by Ron Grainer, who was well known in television circles as a prolific composer of "credit" music for television shows. One of the best known of these was the striking introduction to Dr Who and I wondered how he could produce something suitable for a romantic musical. In the event he turned out a very tuneful score, which many of those who saw the show will remember to this day.

John Clements was to play Papa Barrett. Elizabeth was played by a stage heroine of mine, June Bronhill, whom I have mentioned elsewhere for her scintillating appearances at Sadlers Wells. The leading man, in the part of Robert Browning, was Keith Michell, who was making something of a name for himself on the West End stage.

The rest of the cast was also packed with talent. In her first part since leaving RADA, a young actress named Angela Richards would make a big impression as one of Elizabeth's sisters. Another was played by Sarah Badel, who had a successful career ahead of her in many a television drama and was, incidentally, daughter of another fine actor, Alan Badel. Jeremy Lloyd, who played Captain Surtees Cook, had worked as an entertainer in cabaret, but became better known later as the author of successful television sitcoms, including Are You Being Served and 'allo, 'allo.

A fine actor/singer Charles West played the doctor who attended Elizabeth and his part was expanded to include the reprise of one of the show's principal numbers. This was fortunate for me because I understudied him. He understudied John Clements so that when either of them was absent I stood in for Charles, something that happened quite frequently in the course of a long run.

John Clements' co-director was Wendy Toye, who also choreographed. She was a very talented dancer and although obviously no longer in the first flush of youth could get up in front of the chorus and demonstrate the steps she wanted. Many years before, as a child, I had been taken to see a show at the London Palladium, in which famous comedian Tommy Trinder was the leading comic. The climax was a musical number in which the Dagenham Girl Pipers came on stage to augment the pit orchestra. Then, the doors at the back of the auditorium opened and a guard's band in full dress uniform marched down the aisles, making a tremendous impression on my young mind. When I mentioned this Wendy, she confessed that she had choreographed the spectacle.

When I joined the company the show was not yet in rehearsal and I was asked to assist at auditions, which included reading in with aspiring artistes. Having endured so many frustrations at the receiving end of this particular torture, I tried to make them as comfortable as I could, standing down stage, for example, so that they could show themselves in the most favourable light. On one occasion a young actress was escorted through from front of house, instead of arriving backstage from the stage door. She was given a chair on stage, where she sang in a quiet, but not particularly impressive, voice. She and I read a few lines together from a scene involving Elizabeth's sister, then she was thanked for giving her time and led away. Obviously it was decided by one side or the other that there was no part for her. Six months later she took the lead in the West End production of Cabaret. She was, of course, Judi Dench.

The show opened at the Leeds Grand Theatre, a wonderful venue, known as a production theatre because it had facilities backstage for building full-scale sets. The scenery was quite advanced for its time, comprising a number of trucks which it was originally intended should be moved by remote control, but eventually had to be either driven or pushed into place. The show started with a big out-door chorus number "in the vicinity of Wimpole Street". It moved into the hall of the Barrett's house, then its garden, Elizabeth's bedroom, the stage of the Theatre Royal, a place called Cremorne Gardens in Chelsea, and Browning's study.

After two weeks in Leeds the show moved to Manchester, where the management had bad news about the West End venue. The original production plans and budgeting had been drawn up for it appear at Her Majesty's, a fine theatre, with a big stage and an auditorium large enough to ensure financial viability. A play entitled the Right Honourable Gentleman was currently occupying the theatre and was due to be ending its run in time for us to take over. Then we learnt that the management of the play had decided there was still some profit to be earned from it and changed its mind. This was disastrous.

The only other theatre available was the much smaller Lyric, in Shaftesbury Avenue. Drastic alterations had to be made to the size of the stage settings. Two rows of seats would have to be removed to accommodate an enlarged orchestra pit. Of perhaps secondary concern was that there were fewer dressing rooms. Despite this the show was a great success and ran for some three years. The management of Her Majesty's, however, must have been mortified, because its play came off shortly after.

The final scenario of the play was a massive transformation scene to bring the curtain down on a flamboyant note. It opened in the gloom of Vauxhall station, with the characters and chorus in dark clothing. This was followed by the stage in semi-darkness as a miniature train crossed a backdrop accompanied by orchestral music. The journey ended with lights up on a full stage in Florence and the two principals arriving in lighter costumes, accompanied by a chorus of Italians also colourfully dressed. Precise times and careful coordination between all backstage departments were essential. On it could depend the success or failure of the show.

The dress rehearsal in London was played to a public audience and the press. It went well. There were no mishaps and we approached the final denouement with something of a relief. The closing change approached. I checked that all the backstage staff were in place, and watched while the stage manager on the "book" pressed the necessary buttons. Lights down on Vauxhall Station. The cue was given for the model train. Two flats had to be moved aside in the semi darkness. The cord on one snarled on the backdrop, which collapsed revealing the backstage mechanism and a train that refused to move. There were the usual gasps of astonishment from the audience. The lights came up on a somewhat chaotic Florence and a group of actors trying to make something of the final scene. The curtain fell and the applause from an audience presumably trying to interpret what they had seen, was muted.

I sat with my head in my hands, feeling that I had failed and my life's work was in vain. Wendy appeared through the pass door and I waited for the outburst of anger and the news that I had been sacked. Instead, she clasped me in her arms and congratulated me and all the backstage staff. When I pointed out we had just had a scenic disaster, she reminded me of the superstition that a perfect dress rehearsal would mean a disastrous opening night. She had sat through the whole show praying for something to go wrong, and when at last it did she was very relieved. Superstition or not the opening night went perfectly.

So, indeed, did most of the performances. I do recall one amusing incident after we had been running for a while, when members of the chorus came off after a number in hysterics. When asked to tell us what was so funny, they pointed across the stage to an audience box where the percussionist had been located due to the restricted space in the orchestra pit. It appeared that a replacement drummer had been employed for the performance, but he turned out to be physically challenged and could not be seen behind his equipment. All anybody could see when they looked towards the box were the white knobs of drumsticks waving about in the air.

Part of my job was to rehearse understudies. This was a complicated process and it was essential that they should be ready before the show opened. Having got them to performance standard I then had to prepare the second understudies. At one point in the run we actually managed to set up some kind of performance for the approval of the directors.

The real triumph of the show for me, however, was that on many occasions I was required to play the part of the Doctor and sing his number. Charles West would be required to take over the lead when John Clements was off, sometimes because of his wife's serious disability. She was Kay Cavendish, who had been a wonderful, popular actress, with a distinctive voice. Sadly she had been struck down with what I believe was Parkinson's disease and would sometimes visit the theatre in a wheel chair. There were also times, particularly during the winter months, when Charles himself was off, so that I had the privilege of sharing the stage with the great man himself.

Towards the end of my stay with the company I was called upon to take over the small part of a crossing sweeper as neither first nor second understudy was available. He virtually opened the show and established the London setting by sweeping his way across the stage and singing out to the audience a few lines listing various famous London streets. Although I had been rehearsing others in the part for months I had never actually practised it myself and I was facing an audience in it for the first time and with no notice.. As a result I got the streets mixed up and included a few that were not in the script. When I turned to sweep my way off stage I found the chorus lined up behind me, backs to the audience, their shoulders shaking with laughter.

I was also responsible for settling in replacements for the current cast, which began after the show had been running for a few months. During my time there Keith Michel was followed by two of these and June one. Those playing smaller parts were also replaced and had to be rehearsed. John Clements stayed the course for 18 months, but there came a time when sadly we learned he would be leaving the company.

The identity of his replacement was eagerly awaited, but there was some trepidation when we learnt it was to be Donald Wolfit. I had seen him perform many times and regarded him as a fine actor, but he had a reputation for being difficult to work with. Also I was fairly certain that neither he, nor a recent replacement for Charles West would miss as many performances as their predecessors and I would have few, if any, opportunities to take over the part of the doctor. I decided it was time for me to leave.

Chapter 29 - To be, then not to be

Working on Robert and Elizabeth was undoubtedly the peak of my theatrical career, but from the heights of a successful musical I descended into an abyss involving one of the biggest flops seen on the West End for years. In addition I was leaving the company of artistes I admired and who treated me with respect to work for someone who seemed determined to live up to his reputation of being the rudest man in the theatre world.

His name was Peter Cotes. He was related to the well-known film production duo, the Boultings, who reputedly referred to him as "our bloody brother". Otherwise his only claim to fame was that he directed the original production of The Mousetrap in Liverpool. I was not aware of this, however, when I joined him. He had acquired the rights to a play entitled "Staring at the Sun" and had assembled a talented cast, including his wife Joan Miller, Yolande Turner, June Barry, Melvin Hayes, and Andrew Ray, son of the well-known comedian Ted Ray. I was appointed company and stage manager and to play a small part.

It turned out to be a period of profound misery, largely because the brooding enmity of Cotes was directed not only towards me, but to all those involved in the project, with the possible exception of his wife. I never remember seeing him smile, or expressing himself in any other than a derogatory way towards others. My memories include being driven hunched up in the back of his little bubble car, with his wife in the front passenger seat.

One day I was away from a rehearsal on business and returned early afternoon to find the cast sitting around in a semi-circle on stage, confronted by the director. He asked me where I had been. I started to explain, but he cut me off by saying that he did not expect to employ a dog and bark himself. He demanded to know why the cast had gone out drinking during lunch and returned late, drunk and incapable of doing their work. He seemed to regard it as my fault.

The play had a dreadful script, which he seemed incapable of improving. It was a flop both with audiences and the press. Any other producer would have taken it off before the end of the first week, but Equity required that actors should be paid at least two weeks' salary in addition to rehearsal pay. He insisted, therefore, that the actors should earn their money and the run should be continued until the end of the second week, even though it played to empty houses.

It was time for me to take stock. I was in my mid-forties. Robert and Elizabeth had been a crowning success, but Staring at the Sun had shown how easily this could be followed by darkness. I was quite prepared to move in the reflected light of great actors like John Clements, but I deeply resented being humiliated by the likes of Peter Cotes. There must, I thought, be easier ways to starve. The live theatre seemed to be entering a period of depression. The dread box had undoubtedly seduced the popular audience and its arrival in nearly everybody's living room meant that the regular or seasonal fare provided by live theatre, particularly the reps, was no longer required by former loyal audiences. Theatres I played in for a season or touring were closing throughout the country.

The West End itself was changing imperceptibly. It remained one of the supreme cultural centres of the world, but its driving force became fundamentally different. Traditionally it had been directed towards an essentially national audience, for whom it was the primary source of entertainment, aesthetic as well as popular. Visitors to London were of residual interest, but they were not the deciding element in a show's success or failure. Then visitors began arriving from all over Europe, the USA and eventually the world. In an earlier chapter I have tried to describe what it was like in the British theatre, even as late as the 1960s. New plays could be seen on the West End practically every night of the week. The Shavian influence was still strong, producing a combination of 19th century comedies and the solemn dramas of Ibsen and Tchekov. That was not what travellers from half-way round the world had come to see. What did they want? Well, apparently they wanted what became known as the musical.

There is little doubt that I could have had a reasonable career in television, but I did not see myself spending long hours conforming to the demands of directors, cameras and lighting, with the end result a few minutes screen time in a soap, or – even worse – an ad. My love affair, my obsession perhaps, had been with the audience and the opportunities that gave for those on both sides of the curtain to enjoy a live emotional experience. So I decided to leave the professional theatre for good.

I had worked hard and been successful in my way. I had been a leading actor and director on the provincial stage. I had acted, sung and directed on the West End. But I was not in any sense a celebrity. There would be no fanfares of departure. No startled newspaper head-lines, no expressions of regret from disappointed fans. In a Hollywood movie the climax would have been the successful opening night of Robert and Elizabeth, perhaps with me taking over the lead and becoming a star, but this was real life. It was a triumph of sorts, but it was followed by the disaster of Staring at the Sun. My theatrical world must come to an end and, as T. S. Eliot has expressed it so succinctly, it would do so not with a bang, but a whimper

Epilogue

I left the professional stage, never to return. It was the end of an affair, but fortunately an old love was prepared to welcome me back. I had never completely neglected writing and found no difficulty returning to it professionally. I became editor of a prestigious international trade magazine, which led me into a world of travel and exciting industrial and commercial developments.

Then I became involved in an entirely new field of professional activity, but one which coincidentally took me back to my very first job. I was appointed Secretary General of an international trade association with members and member associations in fifty countries. I took full advantage of the opportunities it gave me for further international travel and the organisation of meetings and conventions throughout the world.

At an age when most people consider retiring I became Chief Executive to the Society of Association Executives. This was a rewarding job, which had its challenges, however, as my members were, of course, all doing the same work and probably rather better than I was!

When I was 80 I had a heart attack, followed by a by-pass operation, which fortunately was successful. I decided I should do something to justify my continuing existence and turned my hand to writing novels, producing the obligatory 1,000 words a day stipulated by Jack London if one is to be regarded as a writer!

Over the next ten years I finished about half a dozen, some of which I published on Kindle. One of these, Tiger's Heart, a novel about Shakespeare's "lost years", has been published in hard- and paper-back by New Generation. I am still drafting my latest and if I manage to complete it will have achieved the somewhat dubious distinction of writing my first novel at the age of nine and the latest at 90.

I have called these memoirs Stony Ground, but not with

the intention of complaining at my lot. Rather the reverse. I hope they suggest that regardless of an inauspicious background and the obstacles of fate it is possible to have a good life and make the most of one's opportunities. If I have not fully achieved my potential I have no one or nothing else to blame. As Cassius says: *"The fault, dear Brutus, is not in our stars, but in ourselves that we are underlings."*